Praise for
The Unspoken

"Ashley Haseotes' story of healing is one of strength, beauty, and transcendence, borne of her soulful willingness, understanding, and wisdom. *The Unspoken* is for everyone and anyone seeking spiritual insight into rising above life's traumas and experiences. Read this book and be restored."

—**Michael Bernard Beckwith,** Founder and Spiritual
Director of Agape International Spiritual Center
and Author of *Life Visioning and Spiritual Liberation*

"*The Unspoken* transforms the meaning of suffering from a detrimental emotion into a necessary (albeit unwelcome) step to overcoming the roadblocks hindering success in one's personal and professional life. Kudos to Ashley Haseotes for this achievement and for having the courage to share her story."

—**Dominique Easley,** Former NFL Player,
Super Bowl Champion, and Mental Health
and Wellness Advocate

"*The Unspoken is* a beautiful testament to one woman's journey of transforming confusion and wounds into clarity and love. Healing is the single most important purpose of our Lives here on Earth."

—**Elaine M. Grohman,** Energy Healer, Intuitive,
Educator, Author, and Radio Host, whose Life is dedicated
to helping others understand the true meaning of Healing

"The emerging power after awakening creates immense courage to [pass on] your learnings and discoveries onto others. Recognizing the causes and sources of debilitating trauma, Ashley shows her readers how to overcome it. She lays bare her pathway to inner peace, helping to inspire others to begin their own journey. Welcome Home."

—**Rev. Dr. Temple Hayes,** Mystic, Spiritual Leader,
and Difference Maker

"*The Unspoken* is a powerful example of self-healing in action. Ashley shows us how chronic physical pain and crippling anxiety can be rooted in unresolved psychological trauma and how we all have the ability to transform our lives."
—**Dr. Nicole LePera,** The Holistic Psychologist and Author of *How To Do The Work*

"Healing childhood trauma is not for the faint of heart. Ashley's courage jumps off every page as the reader rides this roller coaster of processing pain and finding purpose in the mental and physical manifestations of it. Her vulnerability invites the reader to consider their own self-examination to reconcile their past and present. The layers of loss surrounding her own son's battle with cancer and the death of her niece break your heart until Ashely stitches it back together on this redemptive journey. A triumphant work of love and loss, connection and abandonment, self-discovery and self-love."
—**Wendy Tamis Robbins,** Coach, Speaker, and Best-selling Author of *The Box: An Invitation to Freedom from Anxiety*

"There are few people in your life that you really connect with the way that Nancy and Ashley did. Ashley is [one of the most] open and honest people you will ever meet, and her story is one that will catch your attention... like she is sitting across from you having a coffee."
—**Taylor Twellman,** ESPN analyst and Founder of ThinkTaylor.Org

"*The Unspoken* is a compelling story of faith, trust, and determination— energies not often present when people face a crisis (or crisis after crisis). Ashley's honesty and integrity speak to the opportunities found when challenges are met with faith and determination. Readers will find inspiration and courage to face life's challenges, which are actually opportunities, knowing that possibilities are available to all when there is trust and belief in your own 'powers,' and you use your will, faith, and patience to continue to move forward. Ashley's honest disclosure of her life experiences solicits a curiosity of what is next... and just at the right moment, the curiosity is met by a reflection of Ashley's courage, strength, and faith, even in the most challenging of times. *The Unspoken* provides inspiration to all as we journey through life's challenges and opportunities, and I highly recommend it!"
—**Rob Wergin,** Divine Conduit

The Unspoken

A Soul's Reflection on Healing from Abuse,
Neglect, and Chronic Pain

Ashley Haseotes

**MADE FOR
SUCCESS**

Made for Success Publishing
P.O. Box 1775 Issaquah, WA 98027
www.MadeForSuccessPublishing.com

Distributed by Made for Success Publishing

First Printing

Library of Congress Cataloging-in-Publication data
AH Stardust, LLC
THE UNSPOKEN: A Soul's Reflection on Healing from Abuse, Neglect and Chronic Pain

    p. cm.

LCCN: 2021947675
ISBN: 978-1-64146-677-6 (*Hardback*)
ISBN: 978-1-64146-686-8 (*Paperback*)
ISBN: 978-1-64146-678-3 (*eBook*)
ISBN: 978-1-64146-679-0 (*Audiobook*)

Printed in the United States of America

For further information contact Made for Success Publishing
+14255266480 or email service@madeforsuccess.net

Contents

Dedication

This book is dedicated to my husband, Ari. I knew when we were just 22 years old that our love was unbreakable. Thank you for loving me so unconditionally and so deeply. This book is because of you and for you. With my deepest gratitude and forever love.

To my children. My love for you could never be put to words. You all are beautiful souls that I am most honored to share this life with. Thank you for loving me; I receive it as a blessed gift.

To my father, I love you.

Acknowledgements

To Anna: I owe my healing to you on so many levels, thank you for every moment you held for me.

To Morgan: You took care of me at my lowest point, and I will be forever grateful.

And thank you to my editing team, I am so grateful for your guidance and input.

Author's Note

Trauma comes in so many different forms that it's near impossible to keep count, and there's not a single one of us who hasn't endured it on some level.

You can experience trauma firsthand, witness another's trauma, or be traumatized by hearing someone talk about their trauma. Losing a job is traumatic. Long-term prolonged job stress and how we internalize and perceive our safety within this confine can be trauma as well. The news can traumatize people, as can movies with deep emotional plots. Even a global pandemic can trigger trauma in some people.

Oftentimes, people don't even have language for the trauma they have experienced. They may simply describe their situation as tough or difficult without knowing that their body and nervous system are indeed traumatized. In fact, that is precisely what I did.

Before we dive in, let's define the word trauma and discuss what happens in our bodies when we are faced with traumatic situations. There is Trauma with a capital "T" and there is trauma with a lowercase "t"—the grammar is relative. However, both are the same; it's a jolt of energy into the human nervous system, and regardless of whether it was capital or lowercase trauma, that energy needs to be released in order for the human nervous system to lower back to baseline. Think about the common light bulb. The energy of electricity turns on the bulb because there is a path of release or ignition—in this case, light—and release is necessary to turn on the bulb. It's also true that if the electricity doesn't have a path to ignition, the bulb will blow up or "pop." Energy always needs to release. It is science; fact.

Humans can have their own pop, and it is often referred to as a breakdown. Breakdowns come in all shapes and sizes; some are seen, and some are not. Our nervous systems are only able to hold onto additional energy in the form of stress or trauma for just so long before the perfect storm happens and then—POP.

The parasympathetic and sympathetic nervous systems are in place within all humans as a way to excite and calm the body. When they are in good working order, our bodies are programmed to have these systems kick in when there is a perceived threat and to calm down when it is gone. For example, let's suppose a brown bear is chasing us. When we realize there is danger, our **sympathetic response** kicks in and we excite in order to flee and get to safe ground. Then, when we are free from the bear, we calm down and rest (**parasympathetic response**). Often people will refer to sympathetic as "fight or flight" and parasympathetic as "rest and digest."

When we see the bear, electrical signals go from the sympathetic nervous system to the brain, and then from the brain to the organs such as the heart, lungs, and muscles of the legs. It is preparing the body to literally run; hence the increase in heart rate and heavy breathing. When the bear is gone, the system goes back to calm—back to homeostasis.

The glitch in these systems is that our bodies don't know the difference between a brown bear, the loss of a job, feeling trapped in a stressful job, an abusive parent or spouse, watching riots on TV, childhood cancer, death of a loved one, or a pandemic. While the bear eventually retreats to his cave (or eats us), an abusive parent, having to bury a loved one, or fear on the news and social media can be constant. Because of this fact, our bodies thus think that we need to stay in sympathetic overdrive. In other words, we are in constant stress.

Stress in our lives increases stress hormones within our bodies such as cortisol and adrenaline. This then diminishes sleep, decreases digestion, changes our hormonal system, makes our liver sluggish, and stops our gut from working properly... the list goes on. If we pump constant adrenaline and are not sleeping well, our bodies are not restoring while we sleep. If we are not digesting our food, then we are not getting adequate nutrition. In other words, constant stress and not healing our trauma makes us (and keeps us) sick.

It made *me* sick.

This memoir is my story of trauma, loss, chronic pain, and spiritual healing. In sharing my experience of healing, I'm tapping into a universal connection that recognizes we are all imperfect humans; we all suffer trauma on some level, and that understanding brings us together. In this book, I share stories of my life and my healing to help you as you find your own path to healing, and I share my transformation to give you permission to transform. I share with you, the reader, my deep, dark inner emotions and my acts of forgiveness so that you may also give voice to your own pain and also forgive.

I share my story so that you can share yours.

Prologue

tretched out on the hospital bed with our infant son, Nicholas, on his chest, my husband was visibly in shock. I paced while waiting for the doctor to come and give us Nicholas's test results. Our baby boy had been sick for weeks, and with each passing day, he was getting worse. He spiked a fever that wouldn't go down, was constantly vomiting, not eating, and moaning in pain all the time. For weeks, all I could do was hold him all day. I even napped with him! He wouldn't let me put him down. The color in his face was draining away, and he just looked so ill. Over the course of several weeks, we went back and forth to the pediatrician's office, monitoring his progress (or lack thereof) closely.

The week prior, I tried to tell Ari that I knew his sickness was serious. My husband thought I was a crazy first-time mother, worrying about things that were not happening. I cried all night during the night before we got the diagnosis, because I felt—deep in my bones and my gut—that something was wrong. My intuition was telling me my child was gravely ill, and I couldn't help but think it was cancer.

The moment the doctor turned the corner into our room with tears in her eyes, I knew it for sure. My little boy was sick.

"Your son is sick," the attending physician said matter-of-factly, "and I have called an ambulance to pick him up to transport him to Boston Children's Hospital."

"Does he have cancer?"

"I think so," she choked. "His white blood cell count is over 55,000. I think he has leukemia. I am sorry," she mumbled as she walked out of my sight.

From the time I was 12 years old, I daydreamed about marrying a tall, dark, and mysterious man. We were to have a love that could never be broken, a love that defied all odds. In fact, in my visions, it was my love for my husband that brought him back to life from a terrible sickness. This daydream often popped into my head while I drove to school, while I was in class, during boring movies, and as I fell asleep at night. I scrolled through every detail of how I nursed him back to life with my love: showing up at his hospital room and kissing his cheek hello, playing his favorite music. I envisioned what I wore, and how I took care of him like no one else could.

Subconsciously, I dreamt this life full of love and triumph as a way for my brain to escape the life I was living; as a way to have something to look forward to. I was desperately dreaming of my happy ending. Fantasizing about a love such as this was a survival game my mind played; anything to not be present with the pain I was experiencing. It was a fantasy, but how I felt when I thought about it was as real as the sunshine in the sky. I felt the fullness in my chest of our triumph against all odds. Every part of my body was involved in these little dreams. I felt the love; sensed it in every aspect of my being. Oftentimes, I was brought to tears in these moments because it felt so real.

For years, this scene played again and again in my mind. It was a daydream then, but that daydream is exactly what happened. Only it wasn't my husband that I nursed back to life with my love, it was my son.

Was it foresight? Did my soul know that this was going to happen later on in my life, so it was preparing me all along with my daydream? Or did I will it all to happen with the laws of attraction?

Our 7-month-old had leukemia—the rare form with the bad odds. Nicholas was in treatment for 188 straight days from May 8 through October 13, 2006. Ari and I were in our very early 30s, and Nicholas was our only child. I had never been so scared and yet, at the same time, felt as if I was exactly where I was supposed to be. I had been rehearsing this in my head for years, and my brain and body knew exactly what to do.

After the emergency room doctor walked out of our tiny room, I turned to face Ari and Nicholas. My husband was white, and if he hadn't already been lying down, I think he would have passed out.

"Nicholas has cancer," he said, barely letting out the words. I placed my hand on top of his, which was holding Nicholas's tiny back ever so gently.

"Nicholas is going to be OK," I said. "He will make it through this, and you and I will, too. This will make us stronger. Our love, our family."

"How do you know?" my husband asked, looking to me for answers.

"I know this to be true the same way I knew he was a sick little boy when nobody else did," I said. But what I was really saying was, *Because I dreamt this day into existence my whole life.*

It would have made perfect sense for the trauma of watching my son fight for his life to have broken me. Everything I saw, witnessed, and participated in during the course of his treatment was shocking, terrifying, and downright inhumane. The nurses even tell you pretty early on that no one can prepare you for a situation like this because the trauma slams both the mother and the father in equal measure.

"It either makes or breaks couples," they told us. It's different than the death of a parent, where you can console your spouse. Having a critically ill child, having to press the code blue button in order to save his life multiple times, holding him down while he fought to break free so the nurses could change his dressings as he screamed and cried, and watching him wither away to barely 15 pounds at almost a year old is a trauma that could break any mother.

It is a trauma that could break any marriage.

Nicholas's cancer was not what broke me, nor was it Lyme disease that nearly brought me to my knees, nor was watching the woman I call mother die after not talking to her for almost 15 years, nor was it her emotional abuse and neglect from my childhood through my early adulthood. It was not, soon after, watching my infant niece fight and lose her life at the same hospital where Nicholas fought for his. What broke me wasn't the loss after loss. No, it wasn't any of those things. It was the sum of them together and the running away that broke me. I was running away from the pain, trying to make it stop, all the while ignoring every voice inside of me that was asking for help. I ran until I couldn't run any longer.

My body just gave up.

I began getting migraines in the summer of 2018. They started off infrequent but quickly became chronic and left me bedridden for most of

2019. Eventually, my migraines became the tool through which I healed. They represented and gave voice to the unhealed trauma I had been storing in my body since I was a child.

When I was at my sickest, I had a migraine every day for almost a solid year before I even got a break for just a few days. Learning to live with chronic pain meant that it was time for me to do the healing I had known I needed to do for years. I had to learn to break down my past, figure out who I was, and put all the pieces back together again.

I will never know for sure what caused the chronic pain, Lyme disease, or anxiety. However, knowing where it came from is not as important as learning to accept my life for what it is and how it has unfolded. I was not good at acceptance; I saw it as failure. I was programmed to fight, to strive to fix and make things better; not to accept things as they were.

I still live with chronic migraines and anxiety, but my life has changed dramatically from what it used to be. I had to find a new normal. A normal that has allowed me to accept my limitations, set much-needed boundaries, see my strengths, and most importantly, take care of my mind, body, and spirit. My journey back to health was long and came with so many ups and downs. Telling this story—my story—was a part of how I healed.

We all have a story to tell.

Part 1

Before

Chapter 1
Relationships

*W*hen you have a critically ill child and live in the hospital, the desire to have meaningful relationships with the strangers around you is immense. More often than not, friends and family either don't show up or don't know what to say that can help. The bottom line is, parents of sick children feel alone.

While getting a packet of crackers and cranberry juice one day, I made a new (and instant) friend. Her name was Nancy, and her son Sean had a very rare and aggressive cancer. They weren't sure how much longer he would live. Nancy and I talked daily, either in the hallways of the pediatric cancer wing at Boston Children's Hospital or by her son's bedside. There was an understanding between the two of us. That's precisely what happens to parents who meet inside the walls of a children's hospital—where there can be few words needed to support a friend; where she knows that I know what she is thinking and feeling.

Nancy appeared to be a rock, strong and outgoing, and she openly discussed the reality of her son's life expectancy. We shared this kinship; people had always described me as strong, too. To the outside world, Nancy and I were unbreakable. But on the inside, we were falling apart.

The two of us talked about what life was like for our families before cancer, how our husbands were having a difficult time dealing with our sons' diagnoses, and how we desperately wanted a glass of wine. I snuck in the wine for us just a few days later and passed it around in paper cups to my friends like it was gold. They received it as such. As the weeks passed, Sean was getting weaker and weaker. His body was beginning to shut down, and Nancy began preparing.

She began planning for her son's death as if she were getting ready for Christmas dinner. Everything was on point. His room was the "End of Life Room" at the hospital, which was reserved for families who chose not to bring their child home to die. It was private, tucked in at the very end of the long hospital hallway. It was always dimly lit, forgoing the fluorescent hospital lights, and part of Nancy's plan was to bring in all of Sean's bed-sheets and comforter from home. She wanted him to be as comfortable as possible as he began his process of crossing over. I prayed with her, I prayed for Sean, and I asked God to watch over Nancy and her husband; for after Sean was gone, I didn't think that their marriage would withstand their loss.

While I was visiting with my parents and Ari's sister the following week in the family visiting room, a nurse came to get me. She turned the corner with a deer-in-the-headlights look on her face.

"Nancy is asking for you," she said quietly. I knew exactly where I was headed. I was going to say goodbye to Sean. I stood up and gained my composure and began the walk to Nancy. I didn't have any idea what I was walking into, which triggered my anxiety so intensely that I couldn't feel my hands, and my arms felt tingly. But my friend needed me, so I pushed through my anxiety and did what I had to do.

When a child passes away, the nursing staff shut off the hallway lights; an indication to the other families to lay low and stay in their rooms. As I slowly walked to Nancy, I recalled the many times we talked about her discussions with Sean about death. Because Sean was worried that he wouldn't be able to find his mom in heaven, they made a meeting place.

"We are to meet in the back-right side of heaven," Nancy whimpered as I walked into their room. I embraced her and we cried together as Sean lay lifeless in his bed.

"Would you like to say goodbye?" she asked.

I sat down in her chair and closed my eyes. "Dear God," I prayed silently. "Please take Sean with you to the gates of heaven. Please watch over his family. They are going to need your support now more than ever." I wiped the tears from my eyes and thanked Nancy for giving me the opportunity to be a part of Sean's life, and be with him at the end. I squeezed her hand and walked out of the room.

My first experience with death was when I was 10 years old, when my grandfather had a heart attack in front of me. Shortly thereafter, my grandmother died. Before I met Nancy and Sean, I had lost five people who were very close to me; three grandparents and two of my best friend's mothers. However, not a single one of those deaths prepared me for Sean's. Sean was 12 years old. He was not supposed to die.

My cousins and I were out to lunch with our grandparents when it happened. Stacie and I were the oldest of the first cousins, and we were together for her brother Chris's eighth birthday. It was February vacation week, and the lunch was supposed to be a kickoff to a fun vacation. We were at one of the restaurants my grandfather built, an Italian place where all the locals ate in downtown Framingham. Everyone knew us—my grandfather was just one of those guys who knew everyone. We were all dressed up, and I had on my dress, tights, and black shiny shoes. I loved to go to the bathroom to hear them click on the tile floor. *Click click.* It made me feel so grown up.

As we all sat there, the air began to change, and I felt the shift in my head. I was getting dizzy and I couldn't quite put my finger on the reason. Then I saw my grandfather put something under his tongue from his pill case. *He uses those little white pills a lot,* I thought to myself. I remember him giving me a bite once. They tasted like sugar.

My eyes were focused on my grandmother, who looked pensive. I was starting to get anxious, and I knew something was wrong. Meanwhile, my cousins were busy eating their buttered rolls. I looked at each one of them, wondering, *Did they feel it, too? The dizziness?* My grandmother put her hand on her husband's and asked him if he was OK, and he nodded yes. He was lying. Sweat formed on his brow, and we all fell silent. Within a matter of minutes, everything changed. Our special date was turning into a nightmare.

And that was the exact moment the chaos broke out. The restaurant staff quickly took us kids out to the empty ballroom in the back. While I was being whisked away, I glanced backward as they laid my grandfather on the floor. It was like a car accident that you try not to look at while driving down the highway. You stare straight ahead until the last moment, when your view is about to get obstructed, *then* you turn your head to see.

I wanted to see what they were doing to my grandfather; what was happening. I would look, then look away. It was all too much. As the EMTs arrived and more people filled the room, I tried to see around them. They moved swiftly, giving him oxygen, taking his blood pressure, and talking to him.

"Ray, can you hear us, Ray, can you talk to us? Do you know what day it is, Ray?"

While all of this chaos was happening, my father arrived. The staff must have called him. They knew my father well because he helped with the construction of the restaurant alongside my grandfather. His big blue pickup truck pulled up and stopped within an inch of the window I was staring out of. He parked on the sidewalk, half in the street, jumped out of the truck and ran into the restaurant. I could see the strain and worry on his face, but at that moment, I felt the safest I had all day.

My mind raced. *Thank God he is here, everything will be OK now, my dad is here.*

I watched as my father got down on his knees beside my grandfather. He untied my grandfather's belt and his shirt, trying to give him room to breathe. It was a delicate moment for me to witness, my father taking care of his father as he was filled with worry and fear. At that point, I don't remember driving to the hospital or where my cousins were. I don't remember talking in the car ride over either. My mind had shut down. It was trying to protect me.

My father and I pulled up to the emergency room, where we found my uncle crying alone in the hallway outside the entry doors. It felt cold in the hospital, like life was missing. I felt sick to my stomach, and as my father stood there, no one said a word. I wanted to go to my uncle, I wanted to hug him, but I just stood there frozen without saying a word. My father did the same. Then, in what seemed like an instant, as soon as we walked in, my uncle stormed off and left the hospital. My grandfather had died.

As early as 10 years old, I remember being able to feel the energy of those around me. I now know that I am an empath, but I didn't figure this out until I was in my very late 30s. I was born this way, sensitive to everything and everyone around me. I could feel the shift in energy of my grandfather the day he left us. His energy was shifting rapidly because he was going to leave this earth quickly, and when that happens, the shift in energy is intense and swirling. It was much different from a person who has been sick for a while and is at the end of life. That energy shift feels a bit more subtle.

It took me months to recover from my grandfather's passing because my body had absorbed so much during that time with him. I didn't know then how to process and release the energy of others. Today, I know how to not only protect my own energy field so that I don't absorb that of others, but I also know how to clear myself if I do pick up other people's stuff.

Learning to live as an empath includes protection of your energy field, setting energetic boundaries and clearing, and, in my opinion, the most important one of all: self-care. Through my healing, I learned that when I witness other people's suffering, my body doesn't know that the experience isn't mine. My nervous system never had the opportunity to reach baseline; it never attained homeostasis after the many crises I endured. Each time I sat at the bedside of a dying loved one, watching my own family suffer, seeing Sean pass, and all that followed became etched in my body like tiny little scars. I absorbed these situations into my body and they got stuck inside.

Every moment, every loss was programming my brain and body that suffering was not only happening currently, but that it was going to happen again and again. The circumstances in my life were training my brain to expect trauma. Every situation I watched, every person I helped through a dark time, and every loss I continued to endure was triggering my survival brain—and ultimately re-traumatizing my nervous system. I was stuck in a post-traumatic state of living for almost 14 years.

The life purpose of an empath is to feel in order to heal.

I know I am not the only empath who has suffered, nor was it being an empath that solely triggered my nervous system to be stuck on fight or flight. In fact, I am convinced that every person who suffers greatly is an empath, sent here to earth not just to suffer, but to use that suffering to heal themselves and those around them. This path of healing is how empaths survive and thrive because, in a sense, that is what we came to earth to do.

The life purpose of an empath is to feel in order to heal.

Chapter 2
The Unspoken

My grandfather was dead. He had a massive heart attack at the age of 60, and I was shocked.

Nothing else mattered in that moment. My world had stopped. I could clearly see my father in pain, and up to this point in my short 10 years, I had never seen anything but a smile on his face. My innocence was lost because death had entered my life. Gone were the days of only worrying about what to wear to school, or if school lunch was going to have ice cream sandwiches for dessert that day. The world had now become real—a new and vastly different place for me.

Though death is a part of the natural life cycle, and none of us can escape that process, experiencing death at a young age changed me forever.

My grandfather and my uncle had *one of those* relationships. The kind where you can feel the tension under every word they spoke. Even at 10 years old, I could tangibly feel their anger and hurt. My empathic and psychic abilities gave me a power to be able to see people's emotions like they were handwritten in the air around them. I would know what was going on without even asking, and I could sense it all as if the emotions were actually mine. Plus, kids often hear the arguments, and they sense what is being said even when the words aren't clear.

My young heart ached for my uncle, who had just lost his father, but I felt his sadness went deeper than just the fact that his father was now gone.

It was the loss of a relationship that was strained. And thirty-five years later, I, too, would be in the same situation with my own mother

In our Italian family, everything was intense. The conversations were intense, and so was the silence. Though I understood what my uncle was suffering, at that age I had no ability to articulate what I was sensing. He desperately wanted to be loved by his father, and for reasons I would never know, my grandfather struggled to show my uncle the love he was seeking. It was in these moments of silence that I understood my uncle. I could see myself in him. My father appeared to have a stronger, closer bond to his father than my uncle did. I still wonder if that was the truth.

I was in fifth grade when my grandfather died. When I returned to school after vacation, we had to write about something fun we experienced during our time off. The idea of fun didn't register with me, so I wrote about how my grandfather had a heart attack in front of me at our lunch table. Needless to say, the teacher called home to tell my mother what I had written about, as if I was in trouble for writing about what happened during break!

My mother told me that my teacher called, but it was like she was telling me as a warning to stop showing my emotions at school rather than, "Don't worry, honey, your teachers are there for you and they will take care of you." She further explained that she told my teacher to give me some time, as it all just happened.

Message received, I thought. *Give it time, and it won't hurt like this forever.* But I wanted to ask more questions. It was clear my mother didn't want to talk about this, so I dropped it and kept my feelings in check at school. No more writing about what was happening in my life. That was too much for outsiders to take. Got it.

It is difficult to explain death to children. Where did Nono go when he died? Why do we bury his body in the ground and then say we will meet him later on in heaven? Up to that point in my life, I experienced nothing in the way of spirituality. I had not been told that I, too, was a soul, just like the soul they told me my grandfather was when he died.

My parents, who divorced when I was five, didn't let me go to the funeral. I only went to the luncheon at the house after the service. There were so many emotions in my grandparents' house at that luncheon, and I could feel every single one. People were sad, of course. But what I could feel most was the energy *in between* the feelings, which was a weird energy in the room. You know the energy left in the room after an argument—it just feels dense. Have you ever walked into a room and nobody is talking, yet you can sense that people are in the midst of an intense conversation? What we feel in these moments is the shift of energy from one body to another and back again. The unspoken; the in-between.

I sat back on the white floral couch and watched and felt it all. I watched the men drink shots, and the women dote over them from the kitchen. I watched my older second and third cousins sneak wine and go into the basement. It was too much for me—all the people, noise, chaos, and emotions. I didn't feel well. My father took me upstairs and put me to bed in the spare room. I could still hear everything, and I could certainly still feel everything, but being in the room somehow helped me feel protected from it all.

I don't recall sleeping. I was so confused. I couldn't pinpoint what I was feeling inside my body because the energy flowing through me wasn't mine. I was picking up everyone else's emotions, and I was confusing them with my own. Why were people laughing and having fun at my grandfather's luncheon?

I couldn't take it anymore, so I marched downstairs and yelled at them to stop. "Stop laughing, stop having fun. STOP. My Nono is dead, and you all need to stop having fun!"

I was melting down. I was in empath overload.

As an adult, I now understand that mourning includes retelling stories, remembering the good old times. But for me as a child, it was a black and white issue. Death equals sadness, and that was that. I was overwhelmed, and I was picking up on emotions that were not mine. I was grieving my grandfather as a little girl, and I couldn't handle the conflicting emotions of being able to hold sadness and smile and laugh at the same time. I just didn't understand how to hold and experience two polar emotions simultaneously—something that would take me years into my own healing to grasp. And I certainly had no idea that I was feeling everything around me.

I had no idea that I was an empath; a sensitive person. Neither I, nor my parents knew that I had the ability to absorb the energy and emotions of others. All I knew was that my body was freaking out, and I wasn't in control of any of it. My body was freaking out because I was in shutdown mode. This is a protection mechanism for empaths, like an emergency brake of sorts so the system doesn't get too overwhelmed. When this happens, your body is giving you physical symptoms, forcing you to stop, slow down, or get to a safe place.

My family didn't talk much about death, even after we lost Nono. My father read me the book *Freddy the Leaf* by Leo Buscaglia, and that was that. We moved on. So, when my grandfather started appearing to me a few months after his death, I didn't tell anyone. At first, when my grandfather appeared, he would be in the yellow bathroom off the hallway, near the bedroom where I would sleep (sometimes) at his house. He would simply stare at me and then disappear. Other times, he would appear at the top of the stairs, stand there, and tie the strings on his bathing suit. I wanted to tell Nona that he was there with us, but I couldn't figure out the right way.

As I grew older, I would see him driving his blue Lincoln Town Car. I would follow him for miles, towns and towns away. It was my grandfather, his salt and pepper hair blowing in the wind, the tissue box in the back window, his big, brawny hands on the steering wheel. I would weave in and out of traffic trying to catch him, and when I would finally pull up next to him at a red light and look over, it would be someone else. I was heartbroken. These appearances went on for years, and one day, they just stopped.

Do loved ones who have passed actually come and visit us, or do we conjure them up in our grieving minds? I didn't think much about all of this until I got older and it happened again and again. Seeing my grandfather was the beginning of being able to connect to the other side. I was born with psychic abilities; I was born sensitive. I later on learned to harness these gifts, but for years, I lived in a state of overstimulation.

It still catches me off guard today when I can smell the incense of the person I am on the phone with, or when the phone rings and I know exactly who the caller is going to be and why they are calling. I know when people are pregnant as early as five weeks, when they haven't told a single person. I hear voices when I meditate, and can easily slip into the other side while I sleep. Following my grandfather in his Lincoln Town Car was nothing.

I had no idea what was coming.

Chapter 3
The Light

My mother's mother died shortly after my grandfather, very suddenly, and it was the same elephant in the room. I felt that weird energy in my body.

What were these adults trying so hard to hide from us children?

The anger was palpable. In both circumstances, the adults were angry with one another. They were angry at others who either said the wrong thing or didn't say anything. I can vividly remember the conversation between my uncle and my mother the evening after they buried their own mom.

"Can you believe she had the audacity to show up here tonight?" my mother complained to her brother. They had both been drinking all night, and she was referring to her ex-best friend. From the time I was little, Judy had been my mother's best friend, and then, one day, she was not.

"Fuck her!" he said. "She doesn't deserve your friendship anyway."

I found their tone to be disgusting and my body revolted listening to them talk with such anger and hatred. Perhaps it was the alcohol that made them use such ugly language. Or, perhaps I found it ugly because I never got to express my own anger, and I named theirs ugly because I didn't know what to do with mine.

I was only 12 at the time, but my anger toward my mother was building and I had no clue what to do with it. It was confusing to both love and hate my mother at the same time. I never told anyone about my feelings, though, and I simply allowed them to fester inside my body.

It was at my friend Alexa's mother's death when I started to believe that we are a soul and come back into a human body more than once. I was 22 years old when Linda fought and lost her battle with cancer, and it had me questioning what my Catholic religion taught me about life and death.

I didn't talk about what I witnessed with Linda until almost 15 years later. I hid it from almost everyone, including Alexa, one of my oldest and dearest high school friends. When her mother got sick, it was like my own mother got sick. I actually liked Alexa's mother more than I did my own, and we were both devasted when she got diagnosed.

As I sat on her bed while she was in and out of consciousness during the last weeks of her life, she talked to her old friends and family who had already passed on. Her conversations with them were very clear. She told them how amazing they looked, asked them where they had been, and then she would cry and rock herself in her bed, like she was hugging them. When she would come back to her physical body and physical space, she would ask us, "Did you see Bob?" Bob was her friend who had passed on only a few years earlier.

"He looks so good; he came for me. He came to bring me home," she would say. "We are going to go together. I love him."

I have been at the bedside of a handful of people at their end of life. While it appears they suffer badly at the end, with rigid breathing and nearly lifeless, hollow body, I now know this is simply their physical body struggling. I know this because the light comes to get them days before the final suffering. I have seen it over and over: with my friend Julie's mother, Alexa's mother, my mother's father, my dad's mother, my stepmother's mother, and most recently, my own mother.

The soul crosses over the week of the light. People come in and out of consciousness while their physical body struggles to keep them alive. When it appears they are out of consciousness, they are on the other side, visiting loved ones and connecting to their souls at a higher level of consciousness. I watched as almost all of them described how their loved ones came for them.

My father's mother was not a very happy woman. In fact, she was sad most of the time. My visits with her when she was living in the nursing home were usually short. Short because I felt jumpy while there visiting her, and short also because she was a woman of few words. When she was at the end of her life, she smiled more than she ever had before. She talked with her friends like they were alive, visiting her just as I was. I sat with her quietly while she was visiting with them, and I was in awe. I remember feeling buzzing in my body, and when I left the nursing home, the hallways always felt smaller and the lighting looked different.

When humans die, they leave behind their energy, also referred to as spirits, and they feel heavy to me. Their energy is so big that it feels like it is pushing me out. I feel a very dense pressure in my head when I am around spirits, and oftentimes, I feel dizzy.

I know today that when I feel these sensations, I am in the presence of a spirit or spirits. However, when I was visiting Nona, I didn't know what I was experiencing. I would walk down the hallways in that nursing home hoping to get to my car in one piece. I had no idea that what I was feeling was the energy of those who had passed while in that very nursing home, or the spirits of friends of the dying. There are spirits around all of us all the time, so for an empath like me, even going to the supermarket can pose an issue. I can feel spirits whenever and wherever I go.

When I was 14 and in love for the first time, my mother's father died of cancer. I don't remember it being a long and awful battle, as cancer can sometimes be, but I do remember the week of his crossing over, the back-and-forth visits by everyone. The food on the table that sits out all day and no one eats, the nurses answering questions like, "how long" and "can he hear us." The questions that even the most experienced nurse can't answer because our death is as unique as our lives. We all go out on our own time and on our own terms. Yes, even the motorcycle accidents and sudden deaths. I believe those are their own terms, too.

What was happening to me during all these deaths, funerals, and wakes was that I was beginning to hone my emotional intelligence skills. I was experiencing life events that are common for adults but not typical for young children, which meant that the feelings I was also experiencing were a bit larger than my psyche knew how to handle. It was on the job training at the highest level. I was feeling the wide array of emotions that people were not expressing, and it was giving me the knowledge of how people acted in contrast to how they actually felt.

For children, hiding feelings isn't commonplace. We have to be taught to hide feelings because it is not the natural instinct of the soul to hide. Rather, the soul wants to share; this is how it grows and thrives. The gap in between what these people felt and how they acted—those were the emotions I could read. I can still do this today. I am able to name what people are feeling when they are trying so hard to hold it in. This ability was what made me a great healer. I could help people express their emotions by coaxing these out because I knew what they were hiding.

The death and suffering I had witnessed was building my toolbox of experiences that would later be useful to me when I worked with clients who were trying to heal. I was making mental notes, and I was listening to the unspoken words.

Having psychic abilities is a gift and a curse for me. I never really wanted to be psychic. I had no plans of opening up a shop and reading people's palms for a living.

As I've briefly touched on already, I struggled with this gift for a long time before I actually knew what was happening to me. I was so sensitive to everything that I did anything I could to shut the outside world off. I would daydream, make pictures in my head of the clouds in the sky, stare at strangers around me while guessing what their lives were like; anything to not be present with all that was swirling around me. I drank too much in high school, and as I grew older, I started running away from everything, while masking my anxiety and pain with the appearance that I was running toward my goals of becoming a successful woman.

The overstimulation of the energy around me, in addition to my own conflicted emotions, became anxiety inside my body, and I used it as fuel to keep pushing on—to keep running.

The gift of being an empath and having psychic abilities was that I can (and do) help a lot of people who are suffering. The curse is that I can feel everything. This means I need to do five times the amount of self-care the average person gets away with. I didn't figure this out until I was in my late 40s, which meant that for almost my entire life I lacked the self-care that I needed to survive and feel well.

While being an empath is a gift, it is one that needs special care instructions that very rarely come with the package.

Do you feel everything around you? Do people call you sensitive? Do large crowds, bright lights, and loud noises send off alarms in your body? Furthermore, do you know how people are feeling simply by being around them? If you answered yes to any of these, you are likely an empath, too.

While the special care instructions likely differ for everyone, you will see how this played out in my own life in the following pages. These are the instructions I wish I could have known when I was in your shoes, and now I give them to you.

Once I began practicing energy work regularly on my clients, I noticed that there was a common theme. When I have my hands on a person, my empath and psychic powers are electrified, and I receive downloads of information from the Universe. This was a gift for them as well as for me! These messages were profoundly healing.

Over and over, client after client, I would hear this knowledge come to me in hundreds of different ways: We are all sent here to earth to figure out our lessons. We agreed to these lessons right before we came into our physical bodies. When we are in spirit, we have a conversation with our Creator, and we recapitulate our previous life and take from it the lessons we learned about love, death, betrayal, family, loss, money, and relationships.

You know, all the big ones.

We gather up all of what we experienced and then agree to our next life. We say, "OK, I am willing to go back to learn the following, and here is all that will take place to create what I will endure. OK, sign me up." And POOF—off we go, never remembering that we *chose* to live this life for the greater healing good of ourselves and those we hold close.

We choose our lives, the people in them, and the lessons we learn, yet we forget that we agreed to all of it; hence our suffering. Can you imagine if we all lived knowing that we indeed did choose the life we are living, and that it is unfolding exactly as it was planned?

A gift was given to me for my clients by the Universe, and it is the knowledge of life's purpose and plan for each of them. I relay this message to my clients at the end of our sessions. For example, I say things like "Indeed you chose this life; indeed your brother is here in this lifetime to help you, and here is how."

Knowing the reasons for things is how humans trust, and receiving this knowledge often helped my clients to be more open to trusting the Universe on other situations that they didn't have the answers to. These little nuggets of information were what kept my clients going; kept them on their spiritual paths. How different would it be if we all knew for certain that every single experience in our lives was happening exactly as it was intended to? Now *that* would be freedom. That would be living in the present moment.

Chapter 4
Breadcrumbs

As young as 12, I began to feel a deep sadness building inside me. As I got older, I think everyone close to me also knew, and frankly, I wasn't even trying to hide it. I told my friends when I was sad, I didn't hide my mother's neglect, nor did I try to pretend that she wasn't emotionally abusive to me—although I *did* try to bury the later shame throughout the many years I dated men who lied and cheated on me.

My closest friends knew I was in pain. I allowed myself to become vulnerable with them, sharing my feelings of embarrassment and humiliation. I would get drunk and cry almost every weekend, while my friends (literally *and* figuratively) held my hair back while I puked. For everyone else, I covered up the shame with a thick wall of "I don't give a fuck." I was simply keeping up appearances.

As a young woman, I endured years of embarrassment knowing that two of my boyfriends were cheating on me. It was hard enough being a young woman and finding my way through life, and dealing with big emotions like shame were too much for my young mind and body to handle. At that time, I didn't know the first thing about how to feel such intense emotions, let alone release them. I didn't know back then that it was a lesson that I indeed signed up for. It just felt awful, and what do teenage and young women do?

We wallow in feeling awful.

Shame is one of those emotions that we are hardwired to hide from the world, and I felt deep shame for staying with those boys. Furthermore, guilt is shame's cousin, and they travel together all the time. The guilt that came from beating myself up for staying in these relationships was immense. I was angry at myself for not getting out, but I hated myself for how weak I was for staying. And that brought about the trifecta of shame, self-hate, and isolation.

Though I didn't try to hide my pain, I was never truly honest about how I felt about myself. I never told any of my friends that I hated myself for staying in those relationships. However, my anxiety was bubbling over the top, and I let that emotion out easily. In fact, wearing my anxiety like a warm jacket was my superpower. There is something about sharing my worries and anxiety with others that makes me feel lighter. Even today, I'll tell the stranger next to me in the supermarket that the crowded line makes me anxious. I am free to be open that my marriage isn't perfect (because many people think it is), or that I know my anxiety made me sick.

Being open was not a problem for me; the *knowing* what was inside of me to share was the tricky part. I was not in touch with the (many) hidden emotions I buried down inside me. Since I worked really hard at ignoring all of that for so many years, recalling them later on in life was incredibly difficult for me. I had to pull them out.

I can talk with ease about the emotions that lay on the surface of my body and mind. The emotions that lay there can quickly and easily be named when answering questions such as, "How do you feel about this" or "When you think back to such an event, what emotion comes up for you?" These surface emotions are easily found because sadness, hurt, and loneliness are somewhat common and readily talked about. But shame, guilt, abandonment, or crippling fear are not our average emotions, nor are they easily discussed by most. These are not "mainstream" emotions, and most people don't learn how to pay attention to them, nor are they given permission to share.

My beloved TV show in the 1980s, *Sesame Street*, didn't have Big Bird and his pal Snuffy talking about the shame they felt, but they *did* discuss sadness often. In my family, we simply did not talk about our emotions. My mother never once told me she was upset, sad, angry, or any other emotion that I could clearly see she was experiencing. I was taught not to discuss how I was feeling, not only through my mother's own lack of sharing, but also through how she treated me when I *did* share how I was feeling. She continually gaslighted me.

The emotions we learn from our parents as young children give us permission to feel as adults, and because of my upbringing, I was afraid to face the big emotions. Feelings of abandonment, shame, guilt, unworthiness, and conflict—they were too hard for me to talk about, so I buried them deep inside, far down in my subconscious.

Consciously, I could tell you I felt alone, but I would struggle to explain that it was because I felt abandoned by my mother.

Consciously, I could tell you I felt badly about myself for staying with these boys who constantly cheated on me and lied about it, yet I couldn't tell you that I stayed because I didn't feel worthy of anyone better. I certainly could not make connections as to *why* I felt unworthy either. However, I know now that it was my unmet needs that festered these big emotions. It was my need to feel loved that kept me dating a liar. It was my need to be cared for that allowed me to accept their behavior over and over again.

Later on in my healing, I learned how to make the connection from emotion to unmet need. For years before I got to that point in my healing, these big emotions festered like a chemistry experiment ready to explode at any moment. All it would take was the addition of the wrong element, and *boom.*

In 2012, while getting my hair done, I saw a sign that read "Does your energy need balancing?" I answered in my head, "Um, hell yes it does!"

Being at that hair salon always made me feel like I was going to pass out, totally panicky, but for years, I'd attributed this to my empathic tendencies. I figured I was picking up on all the energy of those around me. I mean, who doesn't talk to their hairdresser like a therapist? But it wasn't until I began putting the puzzle pieces of my emotions back together in my late 40s that I came to understand why I hated the hairdresser so much.

I was 10 years old, and my father was taking me to Hawaii for a vacation the next day. My mother had scheduled me for a haircut at her friend Karen's house. Her daughter Michelle babysat me sometimes, and I liked them. They lived close by, and her salon was in the basement of their house.

I sat down in the chair, excited to get my hair trimmed for my Hawaii trip. I had never been on an airplane before, so it was a big first for me.

"So, we are going to cut it all off," my mother said.

Karen looked at my mother in shock. "Cut it all off?" she questioned.

I had shoulder-length shiny dark brown hair. It was the one thing about me that I actually liked as I entered puberty. My body had begun to change without my permission, and I hated looking in the mirror. I was the first of my friends to get boobs and hips, and I felt like the ugly duckling.

"CUT IT ALL OFF!" she yelled.

I now see that my mother was punishing me for going on vacation with my father, and cutting my hair was how she evoked her control over me. I started to cry, begging my mother not to do it.

"Please don't do this," I cried, "I don't want short hair. Please Mom, don't do this."

She tried to get me to stop crying by offering to get my ears double pierced as a "prize."

"I don't want my ears double pierced," I said, "I want to keep my hair!"

I don't know how Karen cut my hair while I sobbed, but she did. She cut it to look like a 10-year-old boy, exactly as my mother had instructed her to do. I vaguely remember hearing my parents arguing the next day that my mother was going to call me in as kidnapped; hence the haircut. I don't think she ever did. It was so short all over that it wasn't until high school that I could use an elastic again. No wonder I hated the hairdresser. My body was remembering a time when it felt out of control.

As I sat in the salon chair 35 years after the hair-chopping episode, looking at the "Does your energy need balancing" sign, I was feeling dizzy, tired, and scared. With hair dye in my hair, I picked up the 5 x 7 plastic sign and walked to the front desk and asked, "Where do I get this done?"

At that moment, my path for healing was being presented to me.

Once my hair was dry, I waited to be brought upstairs to the spa part of the salon—the place where my energy was going to get balanced. In just those few short minutes, from the time I read the words to the moment I laid down on her table, my life was changed forever. I had no idea what to expect, and part of me was extremely nervous. What would she see? Will she know everything about me? What will I feel like? Will I lose my mind? At the same time, I felt pushed by an outside force. It was one of those decisions that seem like they're making themselves through you and for you. Moments like that happen so quickly that they pass before you have time to reconsider.

Before I knew it, it was happening.

My heart was pounding as I lay on the massage table. I silently wondered if she could see my heartbeat move my shirt. She began working, and her hands felt heavy and cold on my shoulders. At the same time, a wave of warmth flooded my whole body. I felt like my body was a part of the table, and instantly I was terrified that I was having an acid flashback. Before I had time to beat myself up for dropping acid at the Grateful Dead Concert in Boston, back in 1995, I began seeing movies in my head.

With my eyes closed, faces of people I knew and of people I had never seen before were flashed in my mind, in living color. I began to cry, and although I had no idea exactly what I was crying about, I felt gratitude, acceptance, love, and wholeness. I had never felt such peace before. It was as if I had come home to heaven. Once the feelings of love and wholeness settled in, the movies began to shift. I saw scenes of my childhood, but it was as if I were viewing them from 10,000 feet above my own body. I was confused, and yet everything made sense at the same time.

Without the certainty of knowledge, I sensed an understanding of why my mother was screaming at me and making me cry. I watched these movies without feeling the pain, and a level of understanding came over me that provided a sort of weird comfort. As I slowly emerged from the vision, I noticed that I was ugly crying, my bottom lip was curling, my eyes were puffy, and I had snot running down my face. I was falling apart on the table with this strange woman, who was now handing me a tissue, telling me that the tears were a totally normal response to energy healing and that I shouldn't worry.

"Let them out," Lucinda, the healer said softly. My session was 45 minutes long, but it felt as if I had been under her spell for days. Lucinda was and still is an angel walking among us, in my opinion.

After we were done, I sat up, and she asked me how I felt.

How do I feel? You mean, like I want to get the fuck out of here and fast?! What just happened to me?

She gently shared with me what came up for her during our session.

"Who was the woman with the curly brown hair pointing her finger at you and yelling?"

I was shocked. *How did she know this?* My mother had dark, curly hair. Lucinda knew almost everything about me: how I think, what I think, the burdens I carried—all of it. While she sat in front of me, so easily describing private parts of my life to me, I was floating, my whole body was vibrating, and it was freaking me out.

I left there thinking I would never go back.

For weeks, I had a comforting feeling, and I was at ease for the first time in years, perhaps my whole life. Think of it this way: We don't know what warm water feels like if we can't feel cold water. Similarly, we don't know how anxious we are and what that feels like in our bodies until we no longer feel it.

Slowly, the calm and comfort I'd carried around since my session with Lucinda began to wear off, and my anxiety began creeping in again. For those few weeks immediately after my session, I felt on point. I felt grounded and calm, and I felt like I was in my body for the first time in years. My vision was clearer, like I had on new glasses. Colors looked brighter, the world was more vibrant, and my mood was almost elated. I felt strong and full of energy, with enough to go around. Then, suddenly it began to fall off and the elation started to wane.

I have had anxiety since I was five years old, it started when my parents got divorced. Things like stomach aches, tight muscles, dizziness and headaches, foggy-headedness, and mood swings all felt like normal sensations to me. It was only after my session with Lucinda that I became aware that these sensations and sickly feelings were abnormal. In that session with Lucinda, I had been filled with the light and I noticed the contrast. The waning was like a slow progression, symptom by symptom, until I was right back where I was pre-Lucinda.

I began to have weird pains in my abdomen, dizzy sensations in the back of my head, and my energy was slowly fading. The feeling of anxiety and weird sensations in my body made sense to me, so I wrote off the return of the symptoms as my normal—my baseline.

At that point in my life, I was spending almost every day at Boston Children's Hospital with my brother and sister-in-law, BJ and Tiffany. Their infant daughter Evi had been in the cardiac ICU since the day after she was born. I was reliving the nightmare of living in the hospital with a very ill child. I had not even begun to fully process the trauma of Nicholas's journey yet, and now, I was back in the same hospital watching my niece fight for her life. I was helplessly watching my family in pain.

We didn't know then that Evi would never leave.

Healers are not made; they are born. We hone our skills with time, but you cannot turn a person who was not destined to heal others into a great healer. It is a calling, one that you hear in the fleeting moments of clarity during the darkest times of your own suffering. I don't know a single healer that has not endured their own kind of deep pain, suffering, and loss.

At that point in my life, I was starting to sense that my journey thus far was for a purpose—maybe to help others heal. To be honest, helping others heal was simply a distraction for me. If I was too busy helping others, I could excuse pushing my own healing aside. I used the pain I was bottling up inside as emotional intelligence to become a great healer; to become a "good girl."

Healers are not made; they are born

I was learning from the books I read, the classes I took, and I was retaining the knowledge that everything happens for a reason; but I wasn't getting it on the insides of my body, in my gut. I knew it was true, but I was in resistance. I was in denial. But every cell in my body wanted to be OK, and I didn't want to be broken.

Nothing here, folks, keep walking. I am fine!

I was lost personally, but as a healer, I had so many answers. The problem? I couldn't see myself in my clients; I couldn't see myself in the suffering of others. I knew we shared the experience of suffering, but I thought I had passed mine by. I thought I had skipped through and onto the helping others part. On paper, I knew I had suffered, but I didn't think my past was affecting me the way it was my clients. However, Spirit, God, The Universe—they were talking to me through my clients.

"Listen," they said. "These messages are for you also."

I believe we are all one, born from the same source of energy. We are differentiated by our human forms, personalities, and egos. So, when we hear our spiritual leaders preach to us that we are all one, we know that is true. We are all fractions of the same element, The Universe. So then, we are The Universe. Our souls are the purest form of The Universe, as they are without differentiation.

When we meditate, we connect back to our souls and get as close as we can to our purest beginning, The Universe. The soul lays the groundwork for us to experience the gift of our own healing. Then, as a calling, we share our story of healing with others to help them heal. Many will seek it without even knowing they are on a mission of seeking. Like breadcrumbs thrown to a bird, The Universe will create a trail of lessons, opportunities of pain and growth, all leading us toward our own healing.

My belief and the teachings of others such as Buddha, the Dalai Lama, Deepak Chopra, and many others is that every human is on a path back to their soul. We come to earth to learn and grow. We do this mostly through suffering.

It was time for me to be honest that I, too, was suffering. I, too, had pain, and I, too, was broken. I was just like my clients.

At a meditation retreat I took with Deepak back in 2020, he made the entire group of over 500 people laugh when he said, "We are all spiritual Beings, and earth is our rehab." In a nutshell, he is saying that we are here to deconstruct negative thinking, learn to love ourselves, feel abundance and joy, and most importantly, as souls we come into human form only to find our way back to our soul. Over and over again. This is the game of life—to become human so we can experience life for the purpose of remembering our soul. It is an exhilarating game, and it can be a fun one if we let it be.

That day at the hair salon I had taken my first real step in healing. My soul was leading me, and I was ready to follow.

Chapter 5
Plans

Have you heard the saying that God laughs when we make plans? Well, if that's true, then he has been hysterically laughing at me my whole life.

From the time I was little, I would dream and plan. I planned how to get out of my abusive household and dreamed about being a successful businesswoman who didn't need anyone. And, I always dreamed that I would be saved by a man who loves me more than anything.

My making plans was a survival technique I subconsciously used to escape my current life situations. I also felt in my heart of hearts that I was here on earth to do big things, and I was convinced that God allowed me to endure the suffering I had because it would prepare me to best help others through their own suffering. It was almost as if I took each blow, each life event as an energetic hit, got back up and said, "Good, yes thank you for that. I am ready now to help others."

However, I was missing one key element: the healing part. I was simply brushing the dirt and dust off myself and getting right back up, and in the process, I never attended to my wounds. I thought that was the plan, to just get back up again.

I thought I knew what God's plan was for me.

As Nicholas turned three and after I gave birth to Eleni, I made the decision to use Nicholas's journey to make a change in the world. I started a charity, One Mission, and I was working overtime to get it off the ground. In fact, I believed that through One Mission I was carrying out God's plan for me, to help his people. Why else would God give me a sick child if for no other reason than for me to help those families with children still in treatment?

I became hyper focused on carrying out what I believed was the plan God and I agreed to, but all the while I was wearing horse blinders. I saw nothing else except needing to build the charity and help my people. I never saw my own need for healing; I only saw other people's suffering and heard that as a call to help. This is a theme that would come up for me over and over again; helping others before myself. It took me months of therapy to unravel why I felt such a deep call to help those around me who suffered.

Have you heard the parable about the man stuck in a flood who was praying for God's help to be saved? Here's the story:

> A man was trapped in his house during a flood and began praying to God to rescue him. He had a vision in his head of God's hand reaching down from heaven and lifting him to safety. When the water started to rise in his house, his neighbor urged him to leave and offered him a ride to safety. The man yelled back, "I am waiting for God to save me." The neighbor then drove off in his pick-up truck.

> The man continued to pray and hold on to his vision. As the water continued to rise in his house, he had to climb up to the roof. A boat came by with some people heading for safe ground. They yelled at the man to grab a rope they were ready to throw and take him to safety, but he told them that he was waiting for God to save him. They shook their heads and moved on.

> The man continued to pray, believing with all his heart that he would be saved by God. The floodwaters continued to rise. A helicopter flew by and a voice came over a loudspeaker offering to lower a ladder and take him off the roof. The man waved the helicopter away, shouting back that he was waiting for God to save him. So, the helicopter left. The flooding water came over the roof and caught him up and swept him away. He drowned.

When he reached heaven and asked, "God, why did you not save me? I believed in you with all my heart. Why did you let me drown?" God replied, "I sent you a pick-up truck, a boat, and a helicopter and you refused all of them. What else could I possibly do for you?"[1]

The man was so stuck on what he thought the plan was that he missed all of his opportunities for help. Correspondingly, I was so hellbent on thinking I knew God's plan for me that I missed the underlying reason God was sending me my pain and suffering. Like the man in the rising water, I thought I knew God better than God knew me.

God was not sending me boats or helicopters, but he was sending me flood after flood, and for a reason. He wanted me to learn to save myself first! This is a reinforced message that we all hear; you cannot save anyone else when you yourself are drowning. We hear it as a part of the pre-flight safety messages each time we fly—first place the oxygen mask on yourself, then your child.

I never asked God what his plan was for me, I simply assumed. I needed purpose; I needed my life to make sense and for there to be a reason why I endured a childhood full of neglect, and then had to live through Nicholas's cancer. I needed a purpose. I thought I found it in One Mission, so I doubled down.

I was not praying at that point in my life, so it would have been impossible for me to be privy to my plan because I was not even conversing with God. And, to be honest, I was a little angry with the Big Man for allowing Nicholas to get sick in the first place. I saw Nicholas as a flood, I saw my childhood as a flood, I saw being back in the hospital with Evi as a flood, but I just figured my purpose was to have survived all of it. I didn't know at this point in my life that I was a part of an even bigger picture. I thought the goal was to survive, not thrive. I was swimming in my flood, not yet drowning. Time and time again, God was giving me situations in my life in which I could put my own oxygen mask on first.

And he would keep at it until I received his message.

God's plan for me was to be by the side of my family while also taking care of myself... but I missed the memo. I thought God was asking me to

---

[1](https://firefighterssupport.org/the-drowning-man)

suffer again while I watched three people—people I love very much—walk a similar path I had just finished. I understood from all of my floods that I wasn't done experiencing pain, and God had yet to send me a boat. However, I didn't even know to ask for a boat. I was lost in my perceived plan, missing his signs reminding me about self-care. God wasn't laughing at me; he was whispering lovingly in my ear, "Take care of yourself first so that I can keep sending you my other children to help."

We will never really know our plan until we meet with our creator. I will never know for certain why I had to experience such loss and heartache in order to learn to put myself first. I spent countless hours trying to answer this question and many others. The answers were irrelevant, though. It was the process of seeking that provided me all the benefits. I expected that once I got married to the love of my life, everything was going to be easy and full of joy and bliss. I thought I would finally have a break in life, and that my marriage was it. But that was my ego's plan, not my soul's, and I was holding on to that plan for dear life. Whenever I felt as if my plan was getting off course, I held on tighter.

When we get derailed from our plans or experience loss, we can get angry, frustrated, and feel out of control, even lost. Anger is a normal part of loss. We see anger rear its head after the death of a loved one, the loss of a job, or with the failed attempt to make a prestigious sports team. It is acceptable to feel angry in these situations. But what constitutes loss? Does it have to be as overt as death, sickness, or a business failure? Can loss also be defined by the aftermath of emotional abuse or neglect? Can loss be the mourning of a life that we never had, or a plan that never panned out?

Yes, it can.

We suffer when we hold on too tightly to our plans created from our ego self. Loss looks and feels different to everyone, but it always comes down to holding on too tightly. We find freedom when we listen to our souls guide us on their plan—the real plan.

If I were to tell you that the child who endured a life of abuse by the hand of his father would go on to start a charity that helps millions of children learn to break free from their abusive pasts, and many of them go on to have meaningful and successful lives, you may say that the pain was for a purpose—a greater plan.

On the flip side, you may say that the woman who must watch her first-born child fight for his life on the pediatric cancer ward, loses her mother at the same time, and then ultimately goes bankrupt has terrible luck, or even a black cloud following her.

But what if I were to tell you that same woman started a charity that helps families through their journey with pediatric cancer, that the loss of her mother helped her to break free from emotional abuse of her spouse, and that her life in bankruptcy gave her the creative power to build a business making jewelry from home, and that she now earns over six figures? *That* was God's plan.

We often say this phrase, "It was God's plan." We say it (and believe it) when talking about other people, but we oftentimes forget ourselves. God's plan applies to us, and in this, we must realize we don't have full control over the wheel.

The messages that I heard over and over through working with my Reiki clients was that their lives were supposed to happen exactly as they all did. Even the stories that would keep me up at night, stories of loss and suffering, all of it was for the person's best and highest good. It was their life purpose and part of their healing.

Having an abusive mother, a sick son, my own sickness, and being witness to so much loss was my life's dharma, part of my purpose. It was supposed to happen exactly as it did.

You might be asking, "How can loss be for someone's highest good?" I'll tell you why I think that is. Because life isn't a fixed thing; it is energy that is ever-changing. We are all consciousness, and we create our lives from this energy. We manifest a life based on the lessons we agreed to learn before we came into human bodies. It is up to us to be open to the constant change of life.

Don't hold on too tightly and remember that we were a part of mani-festing this plan—our plan with God. We must be in touch with our souls to remember the plan. Going within, sitting with our quiet minds gives us the connection we need to find the guidance and the answers. Going within was how I found my answers and how I learned to loosen my grip, ever so gently, on my plan. Some call this process Enlightenment. The knowl-edge and understanding of who you are, what your purpose is, and what makes you happy. And I believe it is every human's birthright to experience Enlightenment.

It is what we came to earth to do.

Chapter 6
The Angry Lion

*B*reaking habits is challenging for all of us. However, for those of us trying to break habits that were formed over years of abuse, it is much more like moving mountains.

Every day, I am presented with another old thinking pattern that needs restructuring. When I first began this work, the patterns of behavior and thoughts that were holding me back and making me sick were obvious. It was almost easy for me, once I sat down and wrote in my journal, to recognize patterns of behavior around neglect, failure, and trying to be a good girl. I knew even before I began healing my inner child that my mother's neglect affected me in negative ways. This wasn't new or earth-shattering news for me. I could easily talk about how I had anxiety as an adult that was tied back to my mother's lack of nurturing. What took me much longer to articulate and connect was to admit that my mother abused me and that I was angry about it.

If any of what you have read thus far in this book resonates with you, I encourage you to check your A.C.E score online. A.C.E stands for Adverse Childhood Experience, and your score will tell you the likelihood of your childhood having an adverse effect on your adult self. All you have to do is google Childhood Adverse Experience Test. There are many websites to choose from, all with the same test.

Psychology Today defines and separates neglect into four categories.

Physical neglect might mean that a parent is neglecting to provide adequately nutritious meals consistently, or it might mean that a parent has literally abandoned their child.

Educational neglect is a failure to provide a child with adequate education in the form of enrolling them in school or providing adequate homeschooling.

Emotional neglect is consistently ignoring, rejecting, verbally abusing, teasing, withholding love from, isolating, or terrorizing a child. Emotional neglect can also include subjecting a child to corruptive or exploitative situations (such as illegal drug use).

Medical neglect is the failure to provide appropriate health care for a child (although financially able to do so), thus placing the child at risk of being seriously disabled, disfigured or dying.[1]

I would never have told anyone that my mother abused me until 2019 when I began doing this work. My mother only hit me once, so I would not have been considered physically abused, not by any definition. The other aspects of our relationship, such as when she would stop talking to me for months, literally walking by me in our home without even making eye contact, the yelling and verbal abuse, telling me what a bad kid I was and how hard it was for her to be my mother, not attending my school events such as graduation because she was mad at me, or forcing me to cut off all my hair—those experiences were difficult for me to label as abuse. I just thought that I had a shitty mother.

It was my doctor that asked me to take the A.C.E test as a part of my annual exam. I had never heard of this test, and I was actually annoyed that she wanted me to take it. I was scoffing at the idea that my childhood had anything to do with my migraines and other physical issues that I was dealing with in my 40s.

---

[1]https://www.psychologytoday.com/us/conditions/child-neglect

My annoyance was clearly a defense mechanism. I didn't want to be the adult who was an abused child. That thought was too sad for me to accept.

I was shocked when I read my A.C.E. score, and then continued this journey with research on adult PTSD/Anxiety and childhood neglect. I found myself on the pages as I read through the websites, and the emotional abuse section really hit home for me.

I was an abused child. And the aftermath of the abuse was showing up in my adult life as chronic pain, anxiety, depression, and fear.

It felt good to finally have a label for what my mother put me through, and at the same time, it was incredibly sad for me to finally admit. When I told my therapist, Anna, about my score, I began to cry. As she normally did, in her soft and soothing voice, Anna asked me to talk about the emotions that were coming up for me.

"I can see there are lots of emotions that are coming up with this A.C.E score. Can you tell me more about them?"

"It is just so sad," I cried.

"What is sad?" Anna calmly asked.

"It is sad for me to think about a little girl being neglected like that and having a mother who cares more about drinking and being out with her friends than her daughter. It makes me sad to think about a little girl being woken up in the middle of the night on a school night to clean up cookie crumbs from the kitchen counter while her mother screams at her for making the mess," I continued to cry as I went on. "It breaks my heart to think about a young girl waking up on a school day to an empty house, wondering where her mother is. It hurts me to think about how alone she must have felt."

I just kept saying over and over again how sad I was to think about a little girl living a life like this.

"Oftentimes during abuse, we disconnect from ourselves as a protection mechanism," Anna said. "Can you see that you have done this? Can you see you are referring to yourself in the third person?"

"That makes me even more sad!" I cried. "That I am so fucked up over this that even now at 45 I can't even talk about myself in the first person. That is so fucked up."

"What is sad and fucked up about that, Ashley?"

"It is sad that it all happened, sad that I am a mess still to this day, and sad that she is dead, and we will never get the opportunity to fix things between us. It is all just so sad."

"It is sad, and I am wondering if this resonates with you," Anna continued. "The little girl who is sad right now may not have had the opportunity to be sad when she was little. Perhaps that is why you are feeling such deep sadness right now. Should we give her time to tell us her story?"

"Yes, we should," I exhaled.

From there, we let the little girl who was sad tell us her story. I told Anna about how distraught she was to be so lonely and scared in my yellow bedroom at night. I told her that my heart was broken in so many pieces each time I hoped my mother would love me and instead she would drink, ignore me, or yell at me. I told Anna that as I grew older, it was even more sad when I would visit my friends' houses because I would see their mothers love them. My mom hardly ever cared for me or loved me.

I told Anna about the letters I would write to my mother, expressing how confused and sad I was after our arguments. In these letters I would tell my mother how I really felt, pouring my emotions on the page. I stopped writing them after a few years because she would open my bedroom door and throw them at me, telling me she had no idea what I was talking about.

Once the sad Ashley finished telling her story, she told us that being sad made her vulnerable to her mother's wrath, so she stopped being sad around age 14 and became angry instead. She explained that when she was angry, she had protection, and when she was sad, her mother used that as a way to hurt her more.

So sad Ashley became angry Ashley, and angry Ashley stayed for a very long time. Angry Ashley held me up during Nicholas's cancer treatment, and again when Evi was sick. Angry Ashley had power. Sad Ashley had none.

I meet Mary my freshman year at Merrimack College. She was one of the nicest humans I had ever met. She was fun and smart, and we hit it off right away. Mary lived across the hall from me. After a night of partying, we went to our rooms. Soon after there was a knock on my door. I opened it and found Mary standing there with a notebook in her hand.

"I wrote you something," she said as she handed me the notebook and walked away. I sat on my bed and read her poem. It was titled "The Angry Lion."

> The Angry Lion was powerful and all of the animals in the jungle loved the lion, but they feared him more. The lion had a soft heart but he never let any of his friends see that part of him. He roared a lot, and at times, he roared for no apparent reason. This scared the other animals, and soon they began to retreat and not spend time with the lion. The lion grew lonely and sad—he missed his friends. All the animals missed the lion too, but they preferred not to hang out with him because he was so angry. They just wished he would be happier, and they knew that part of him was inside his heart. Years passed and the animals began making new friends, and one day, the lion came upon them in the jungle. They all gave him a passing look but kept on walking, except for one elephant. She could see the lion for who he really was, a warm, kind, and loving lion. Their friendship lasted a lifetime.

I closed the notebook and knocked on Mary's door.
"Am I the lion?" I asked her.
"Yes, Babe, you are."
I cried in her dorm room for hours after that. I didn't want to be angry, but I had no idea how to fix it.

It wouldn't be until I was in my mid-40s that I was even able to admit that I was angry. As I embarked on my spiritual journey, I felt uncomfortable naming my anger for what it was, and I would call it sadness or hurt rather than anger. I was afraid that if I admitted I was angry, I wouldn't also be able to be spiritual.

But the truth was that I *was* angry. I was angry that my mother abused me, I was angry that Nicholas got cancer, and I was angry that my niece was so ill. I thought that being spiritual meant you were happy, but I now know to be spiritual means that you are going within, and if that means you find anger inside of you, then so be it. All that means is that you uncovered the anger, and now you can release it.

I just wish someone had told me that 10 years ago!

My suppressed anger eventually turned into anxiety. Our emotions are energy, and energy that enters your body needs to also leave your body; it must stay in constant motion. If the emotions get stuck, they fester, causing chaos, disease, addictions, panic, fear, and chronic pain.

Without my Angry Lion poem to refer to all these years, I would have forgotten there was a little girl inside me who was angry and needed to tell her story. I pushed her aside for so long I completely forgot she was within me. But she was there, always with me; popping up with the purpose of reminding me I had work to do.

I am usually not a lover of labels; I feel like they never truly describe who a person or group of people are. In this case, falling into the label of an abused child helped me to heal. I was able to see that the emotional torment I endured at the hands of my mother was indeed never my fault. I wasn't a bad child. Rather, she was a sick woman. Putting these pieces together helped me to uncover my true self, the true self who resides deep down inside all of us.

The freedom in knowing that the medical community has studied the impact neglect has on children and the long-term effects when they become adults helped me to not feel alone. It also helped to know that my symptoms of migraine and anxiety, and my fear of pretty much everything isn't who I am; it is a result of the life I survived.

As much as I hated the label, I needed it to give me permission to heal. I took my first step at healing my inner child through learning. We first learn, then observe, and then we make changes. Step by step, up and down, and sometime sideways. Healing is not a straight line.

It is still sad that I can't share this work with my mother. Who knows if she would have said yes to being a part of it? But what matters most is that I am breaking the chain of abuse and emotional neglect and, who knows— maybe by my doing this work my grandchildren will live a normal, healthy life full of happiness, peace, and love!

---

*Anxiety is anger turned inward, or anger repressed. I was afraid
to be angry because I wanted very much to be a happy person.
To be even more honest, I wanted people to think of me
as a happy person. Ignoring my anger made me sick.*

*Is there a part of you that you are trying not to be
for fear of how others will see you?*

Chapter 7
Finding Love, Feeling Lost

From the first time I walked down the white hallways of a hospital visiting my mother at work when I was 12 years old, I knew I wanted to be a helper. I wanted to walk those same hallways as a doctor helping the patients behind the doors. I would picture myself wearing a long white coat, black high heels, and a stethoscope, daydreaming about the people I would help and the long days of medical practice, then going home to my handsome and loving husband and two kids. On the ride home from every trip I took to see my mother at work, this scenario played over and over in my head.

The summer of my freshman year of high school I made the decision: I wanted to go to medical school. However, that dream was stripped away during my first year at Merrimack College. It was chemistry. My brain just didn't understand the language of formulas. Math was my nemesis, so it made sense that I struggled with chemistry as much as I did. I tried so hard—I sat upfront of the mammoth auditorium, and I got extra help. I would stare at the periodic table and wonder, "How do all of you attach to one another?"

One day, after another long chemistry double class, I waited for my fellow students to leave and I walked sheepishly up to the professor as he packed up his bag. "Prof, I just don't get it," I said. "How did you get that other hydrogen atom to move over to the right side of the equation?"

He put his hand on my shoulder and said, "Ashley, I see how hard you are trying, but I just don't think you will make it through this semester, much less be able to move on to advanced chemistry. I think you should withdraw."

As I began to cry, I mumbled, "But I want to be a doctor."

"There are other ways you can help people," he said. "I read your admittance application, and your essay was rich with pain and suffering. You would make a great therapist. Perhaps you should switch your major to psychology." I shuffled back to my dorm that afternoon feeling defeated. My dream of becoming a doctor who would drop everything to help her patients, a doctor who would help her patients heal, mind *and* body was shattered. I skipped my classes the next day, throwing my hands up in defeat. I took to my journal and began to write; about the doctor who I would never become. As I reviewed what I wrote, I too could see my pain clearly on the pages of my journal in words like lost, alone, scared. It was in the dark hour of the loss of my dream where I found a new dream: I could become a therapist.

I withdrew that afternoon and switched my major to psychology. I was thinking that being a therapist was the part of being a doctor I liked the best. When I thought about the kind of doctor I wanted to be, I realized I wanted to help patients through the emotional part of their illness, in addition to fixing the physical ailments. I wanted to help people through their physical pain, but what fascinated me the most—and where I felt I would have made the biggest impact—was helping them through the emotional journey of surgery, pain, and recovery. It was the bedside manner of being a physician that I looked forward to the most.

I left Merrimack after one year, and finished my two-year degree at Mass Bay Community College in Wellesley, Massachusetts. It was there I connected with some pretty amazing therapists who taught classes like Intro to Psychology, Family Systems, Drugs and Alcohol, and Abnormal Psychology. I fit in so well with these classes that things just clicked, and I earned almost straight A's. I graduated Mass Bay and then went on to Framingham State College, now called Framingham State University, to continue on for my four-year college credits.

My sights were set on getting a master's degree in Psychology. I was going to be a therapist.

I worked to put myself through college. My father and stepmother Christy paid for my classes, and I bought my books and paid for my car and insurance. After a major blowout argument with my mother the first semester home from Merrimack, I moved into my dad's house—a move I really should have made (at the minimum) four years earlier when I was in high school.

I had come home for Christmas and I was having dinner with my mother and her new boyfriend. My friend Tanyia was with me. At dinner, I noticed that my mother was wearing a ring that my father had given to me. I thought I had lost this ring months before, so I was both stunned and happy that she had found it.

"Hey, that is my ring!" I said excitedly. "Where did you find it?"

She stared at me blankly. When I asked for it back, she flat out said, "No."

I was flabbergasted. "What do you mean no?!" I replied angrily. "That is my ring! My father gave it to me, give it back to me."

"No," she said, still deadpan.

Having a break from her madness while I was away at school made this moment even more pronounced for me. I had been spending my time with new friends and professors who were all even-keeled, nice people, and I was finally free of my mother's torture. To now be subjected again to my mother's manipulation and evil ways sent me off the rails.

"GIVE ME BACK MY FUCKING RING NOW!!" I screamed at the top of my lungs.

Her reply was evil and calm. "No, you don't deserve the ring. You lost it, and now it is mine."

That was all I needed. I stood up from the table, pushed the dishes off with one fell swoop and stormed out of the house, screaming at my mother, telling her what a psycho she was.

I had never spoken to her about her mental status before; in fact, up until that moment, I had never told my mother that I thought she was crazy. However, the case studies of mental illnesses that I was getting introduced to in school gave me the knowledge I needed to see that she was the one who had the issues, not me. I needed to get out of there.

After that night, I would never return to that home again. I now refer to it as Griffin Road, never as my "childhood home."

I called my father from a nearby payphone and asked if I could come and live with him.

"Peach," my father said, "I have been waiting for this phone call for almost 10 years. Of course, you can come and live here."

And so I lived with my father and Christy from the end of my first semester at Merrimack until the day I got married.

School became my sole focus. I talked to my mother very infrequently after that evening, and she moved to Florida shortly thereafter. I worked and went to school, and I felt happy. Living with my father and Christy was a breath of fresh air, and being in school now versus as a child was a whole new ball game. My focus was actually on my studies and not on the arguments I was having with my mother, or on the cheating boyfriend I refused to leave.

I couldn't wait to become a therapist, and I often thought about what I would call my business and what my office would look like. My dreams were transitioning from escaping my volatile home life to finding my true love, having a job I loved, and living my happy ending.

I took me six years, but I finally left that cheating boyfriend, only to begin a relationship with another shortly thereafter. After the initial breakup, I began dating here and there, but I had not found who I was looking for. I was dating boys, and what I really wanted was a *man*.

In 1997, while I was studying at Framingham State, I met Ari. I worked at a local restaurant, and Ari and his family came in all the time. It took him years to ask me out, and when he finally did he asked me a series of workplace interview questions before popping the question. He came in alone that time, not with his family as usual. After he finished his dinner, he sat with me by the hostess station, since I was running the front of the house for my boss that evening.

I was immediately struck by his aura; his energy was intense yet safe at the same time, and his posture was open. And he was a *man*. He had dark hair that he slicked back, a very muscular body, deep brown eyes, and big strong hands. He wore suit pants, a button-down shirt, and leather lace-up shoes, and I figured he had to be at least five years older than me. I had never dated a guy who wore a suit before!

He kept his hands folded in his lap as he sat in the big armchair, easily asking me questions like "Do you have siblings?" "Did you go to college?" "Do you spend time with your family?" and the big kahuna: "Where do you see yourself in five years?"

Our conversation was effortless, and I could have talked with him for hours not noticing the time. I wanted to tell him my story, I wanted to answer the questions of this tall, dark, mysterious man. After what seemed like a casual conversation, Ari charmingly asked me out.

"Would you be interested in having dinner with me next Saturday evening?" I answered yes before I even figured out that moments before, he had been interviewing me for the date!

We dated for six years before we got married. Everything about both of us is intense: our personalities, how we interact with the world, and, of course, our suffering. I felt the intense burden he carried, and I was drawn to him. Our love was and is still very intense. We both fell hard and fast. I am not sure either of us expected one another to be the last person we ever dated, and although I had been dreaming about him for years, I was shocked when he finally arrived.

My husband has always lived his life by his own plan. I have never seen him waver once from what he set his sights on accomplishing. While we were dating, he decided to go to business school. He had graduated Boston College in three years at the top of his class, and the next step in his academic career was to get his MBA. His dream was to run his family's business, and he was going to stop at nothing to reach his goal. I think meeting me when he did threw a wrench in his designs, as he wasn't planning on me the way I was planning on him.

Ari inspired me to be my best self. It was as if he saw me like no other person on this earth did. He saw potential in me that I didn't even know existed. When Ari got into Harvard Business School, I decided to get my Master's in Psychology as well. His MBA was a two-year program, while my program was three years with a semester of internship. Ari moved to Boston to live on campus, and I got a small apartment just west of the city.

I lived above a coffee shop called The Clever Monk, and I woke up each day to the smell of freshly brewed coffee. My life was a chapter out of a love novel. We would spend our weekends together going out to dinner, drinking too much, making love for hours, until the moment he would have to leave me on Sunday night to go back to school. I would cry for hours after he left, I missed him so much.

I eventually landed a job in the mortgage business to pay for school and my apartment, and I switched to night classes. Life was pretty stable—I was living alone in a cozy apartment, had a steady job, working my way to becoming a therapist, and had a great boyfriend. What more could a young woman ask for?

But it was there, bubbling deep down under the surface. My anxiety was smoldering. I wouldn't say that it was off the charts, and it was certainly lower than it was before I met Ari, but for having all the good I did in my life at that time, my anxiety was higher than it should have been. I was unconsciously entering the phase of my life when I started to run. I was no longer living with my mother, and our relationship was barely alive. Both were a blessing, and at the same time, bizarrely uncomfortable.

I was feeling unsteady, and my nervous system was missing the chaos, the fear, and the preparation for a fight. I was stuck in a hyperarousal state caused by the years of trauma living with my mother. I was feeling off because the torment was gone, and yet at the same time, I couldn't settle without it. I spent my entire life up to this point dreaming about escaping her wrath; about being free.

What I didn't understand was that although our relationship was toxic and hurtful to me, it was a connection, nonetheless. Now that I had moved out and moved on, I was disconnected from my mother in a big way.

Wanting to escape hell and then finally getting out are two totally different things. The inner child would rather have a hurtful connection with her mother than none at all, because even a bad connection provides hope for love.

I knew only one way to live; to survive. I knew how to survive emotional abuse by my mother and my cheating boyfriend. That was a chemical state my nervous system knew how to bathe in, the fight or flight. Fight the wench woman and build walls up against the cheater. However, my nervous system was unsure of how to sit with unconditional love. Ari was unchartered waters. My heart was in conflict with my nervous system to fully accept Ari's love, and I was great at hiding the struggle from everyone—including myself. Because I loved Ari so much and was so happy, I wasn't even aware that my low-level festering anxiety had anything to do with how happy I finally felt. It was a true oxymoron. Per my usual standard operating procedure, I chose to ignore my worries and carry on living the life I had wanted for so long. Pick up and carry on; that's just what I did.

In 2002, five years after we met and the spring of our first semester in graduate school, Ari asked me to take a drive to Cape Cod to check on his parents' house. We took a walk on the beach, and he popped *the* question. I didn't see it coming at all. He had been telling me his "plan" for years: school, work, run the company. Getting married was *not* in his plan, and it was a sticking point for me. I wanted to take the next step and get married, and Ari needed it to happen on *his* timeline. He was worth waiting for, so I waited patiently.

As we were walking on the sand, he stopped me on the beach. "I have something to tell you," he said.

My first thought was that he was going to tell me he was terribly sick, that was how serious the look on his face was.

"How would you feel about spending the rest of your life with me, Ashley?" he asked. I screamed and then cried. We were engaged! Our noses were running from the cold, raw March weather, but the moment was magical nonetheless. As soon as we got in the car to drive home, I picked up my phone and dialed my best friend.

Ari answered. "You are never going to believe this. Ari asked me to marry him." We looked at one another, with the phones to our ears, talking as if we weren't sitting right next to one another in the car.

"Wow that is awesome. Congratulations!" He smiled. Ari was my first call; he was my best friend. He was my everything.

I called my father next. He was waiting for the call because Ari had asked him for his permission the week before. Dad and Christy were so excited for us, and we were all laughing and cheering together on the phone. As we continued driving, dread started to build. I knew I had to call my mother.

This was not an easy call for me to make because we were on and off again talking, and at this point in my life, we were off. I had just left her house in Florida the week before, two days earlier than planned after another argument. I was anticipating her response to be less than enthusiastic because while I was visiting her, she tried to set me up with a family friend, who was a methamphetamine addict. Yes, my mother would rather I date an addict who periodically slept in a slum drug house than marry Ari. You can't make this shit up.

"Mom, it's me. Guess what; Ari asked me to marry him. We are engaged," I said.

There was a moment of silence before she said, without much happiness, "Congratulations, Ashley."

"We are thinking about a June wedding right after Ari graduates next year."

"Will you get married in Florida?" my mother asked. There wasn't a single reason we would get married in Florida; all of our family lived in Massachusetts, except my mother.

I returned her silence, "No, Mother, we are not going to get married in Florida." I was beginning to flail; my emotions were starting to get off kilter and I was responding in rapid fire to my mother's cold response and nasty tone.

"Well, then where?" she asked bitterly.

"I don't know, Mother," I snapped back. "We just got engaged an hour ago."

That was the exact moment the joy of me getting engaged to the love of my life slowly starting to dissipate. My mother took it from me, and then proceeded to make every decision during the planning process about her. What color dress was Ari's mother going to wear? Who was going to walk her down the aisle? Could she sit with me and Ari at our head table? She told me she didn't want my stepmother to be with us while I got ready or at the before photos.

The list went on, and for the next 12 months, I argued with my mother almost daily about my wedding. I cried more times than I can count that year. Against my better judgment, but at a loss for what else I could do, I wrote her one last letter. Again, as I had done so many times in my childhood, I told her how I felt. I poured my heart out in this final letter to my mother, sharing with her my desire to make her happy, while also asking her to meet me halfway. I told her that I was upset that we kept arguing about my wedding day, that it was supposed to be a happy time.

I was desperate for her to tell me that whatever I wanted to do for my wedding day was going to be fine by her, because she loved me and wanted me to be happy. I just wanted her to love me. I explained as best as I could in this letter that I didn't ask for her and my father to get divorced, and that it was unfair for her to put me in the middle, asking me to ignore my stepmother on my wedding day. I asked her to please put her own feelings aside for me—just once.

I waited for days for her to reply to my letter; days of agony worrying about what she was thinking. She finally called, only to tell me that she had spent my entire life putting her own feelings aside for me and that she was hurt that I didn't see that. She told me that she would rather not come to the wedding than have to share any space with Christy, and it was up for me to decide. Then she hung up.

I was frantic and angry; feeling abandoned again and full of fear. I was so worried about upsetting my mother because I feared she would ruin my wedding day if I didn't give her what she wanted. The year of planning what was supposed to be an exciting wedding day was a year full of misery with my mother. Not at all like I had planned.

In the end, I chose me. I told her that I would move the photoshoot to happen at my apartment, so it was neutral ground, but that Christy was invited.

"Your choice," I said.

She showed up late and left early.

Both before I got married and for years afterward, I experienced uneasiness when I also was experiencing happiness. It felt counterintuitive, because it was the same happiness that I had prayed to come to me. I had never been so loved and taken care of before. Ari and I felt perfect for each other, and we were blissfully happy.

Except there was one small tiny part of my heart that was waiting for the next shoe to drop, the part of me that figured Ari would at one point see the real me and leave; the part of me that was so uncomfortable to love and needed him so intensely that I just couldn't let myself be 100 percent happy. This was an unconscious nervous system glitch that played over and over. *Things can't be this good, something bad is going to happen.* Waiting for the next shoe to drop was how I prepared myself for things like my bitter and unloving mother's response to my engagement, or years later, the feared divorce from my beloved.

Years of training my brain and body in this process made it difficult to change, even with time and much effort. I never let myself feel comfortable and safe with love of any kind because I knew it would tear me apart if it got taken away. I didn't believe I could survive another loss like the loss of my mother. My entire life, I made decisions on my safety through the lens of the abuse I endured at the hands of my mother. Not having her love made it impossible for me to trust anyone else's love. I made plans in my head preparing me for loss—all day, every day. This hyper-vigilance is an incredibly common behavior for victims of emotional abuse.

During my engagement, I felt trapped into making decisions that would keep my mother happy. These were decisions I didn't agree with, but I believed would keep her on my good side, and thus keep me safe. I was ignoring my own wants and desires for my wedding day to please the woman who tormented me my whole life. My compass was broken; I was lost in my childhood fear system. I wasn't making sound decisions for my own benefit, rather, I was taking turns at every corner trying to please my mother. Meanwhile, all I wanted to do was crawl up in a tiny ball and cry so hard until my "mother" came to me and made it all better. I was so desperate for her love, acceptance, and some stability in our relationship that I was left feeling lost and worried about what was coming next; feelings I knew very well as we had been doing this dance since I was five. Her "love" always came at a cost.

When parents withhold love from their children, they essentially create confusion and chaos within the child's mind and heart. As a child whose mother almost always withheld her love, I spent my life feeling lost and alone. I was searching for ways to fill the void of her love, and constantly trying to find my equilibrium in life. Even Ari's love was getting overshadowed by my mother's torture. She was bringing me down from the cloud of happiness I had been riding while dating Ari. That is what she always wanted, for me to be down at her level—miserable, sad, and lost.

We all want to be loved. It is a primal need we all share. Uncovering this unmet need while in therapy was like opening a secret door in a funhouse maze. I could see this need to be loved show up in so many parts of my life, and as I healed, I could tie it back to so many emotional moments when my mother withheld her love or flat-out neglected me. I would find faith in love, eventually, and I would trust that Ari would love me forever no matter what. I had to start with realizing the unmet need for unconditional love that existed within me first, and only then would I be able to see how it kept me waiting for the next shoe to drop in my marriage.

During the process of writing this book, one day I wept telling my husband about how this desire to be loved ran so deep within me that it was controlling my every thought. I confessed to him that even as deep as our love was, I feared that if I wasn't perfect, he wouldn't love me anymore. My fear was that if my migraines never went away, he would eventually get to the point where he couldn't live with me anymore. We were out to dinner, and I had tears running down my face. This was a typical scene for us: out to dinner with me crying. Our conversations always ran so deep.

Ari looked me dead in the face and said, "I get it. It makes sense to me now."

He was able to make the connections about how my mother's abuse had impacted me so deeply, and how those unhealed wounds were showing up in our marriage. It was as if the stage lights came on and I was center stage.

My husband *saw* me.

———————

We are all born with a need for connection—to be loved, nurtured, protected and seen. However, many of us didn't have healthy connection as a child, and carry those wounds around today.

Can you identify any unhealed wounds from not receiving love, nurture, or protection in childhood? How are those showing up in your life now?

———————

Chapter 8
The Wedding

*A*fter the grueling year of off and on fighting with my mother, my wedding day was blissful—up until the very end of the evening. Getting ready and taking photos with my wedding party at my apartment rather than my father's house was working out OK. It was super intense with both my mother and Christy in the same small space, but I tried to ignore the energy between them. My mother and I faked our smiles for the photographer. We were doing so for different reasons, but the similarity was that neither of us truly wanted to be with the other. She eventually left and went to the church while I hung back with my bridesmaids.

My father and I rode to the church in an old white Bentley. I felt much calmer just being with him after having made it through the morning with my mother. I felt like I was in the home stretch of the day now; I had finished the difficult part.

I spent months in therapy talking about how conflicted I felt about including my mother in my wedding at all.

"She tormented me my whole life, then moved away when I was 19 years old. It was my father and Christy who took me in after college, so I call *them* my parents. To not have them with me while I get ready feels wrong," I cried to Linda as we talked through it in therapy.

There was a huge part of me that didn't even want my mother at my wedding. All she did was cause me anxiety my whole life. I spent my childhood wondering if she would come home, if she was going to be drunk and yell at me, if this argument would be the last time she talked to me in months. Those were the thoughts that ran through my mind from the time I was eight until my very wedding day. Thoughts like this are beyond unsettling to a child, and they breed feelings of unsafety and fear. I knew how my mother treated me was wrong. She withheld her love, only giving it to me conditionally, if at all. There was always a cost for letting her in, letting my guard down and accepting her love on the rare occasion she was dolling it out.

I didn't want her to be a part of my wedding day at all, yet I felt guilty for even thinking this way. I wanted to leave her behind and start a new life without her in it. My body was filled with such angst. *My whole life.* The year leading up to my wedding was no different, in fact, looking back, I think it was worse. Being stuck in my psycho mother's circus and torture was difficult enough to deal with before I found Ari. Once I did experience his unconditional love, dealing with my mother became unbearable. I wanted to escape her even more, after knowing that there was this kind of love in the world for me.

Meeting Ari and seeing that I could have a normal, happy life and not be ridiculed and manipulated made it more difficult to handle things when my mother would play her mind games. It was such a stark difference: having my mother scream at me, saying how awful a child I was for not seating her up front by the head table, bringing me to tears so many times over trivial wedding details—and then the contrast of Ari's mother, who went along with anything, only giving her opinion when asked. When we can see the contrast, living in conflict is more difficult.

Once I meet Ari at the altar, I knew everything was going to be OK. To be standing next to him brought me a comfort that allowed me to relax and see the day for what it was: a new life full of love and happiness. Our last dance was a group dance-off, with all of our friends in a circle dancing and singing together, all taking turns at center stage. It was the happiest I had ever been. We were drenched with sweat when the house lights came on. We began giving out hugs, thanking our loved ones for coming. As the crowd began to dwindle down, I looked around for my mother.

Maybe she is in the bathroom, I thought. Still looking, I found my father and stepmother. "Have you seen my mother?" I asked my father with trepidation.

"No, Peach, I haven't seen her in hours." My dad kissed me on the forehead as he had so many times in my life. "Tonight was spectacular," he said. "Truly an amazing evening. We love you both so much and are so happy you found one another."

I turned to Ari. "I can't find my mother," I said in a slight panic. Then I found my Uncle Steve, my mother's brother. I asked him if he had seen her. "She left hours ago Ashley," he said stoically.

She left. "Where did she go?" I asked, biting my inner lip to hold back my tears. My wedding night had come to an end, and my mother had left without saying goodbye to me.

I called her cellphone at least 20 times that evening before I went to bed. As I laid down in bed next to my new husband, Ari had to hold me while I cried myself to sleep on my wedding night. Before leaving for our honeymoon in Nevis two days later, I called my mother another handful of times and left messages apologizing, telling her I was sorry if I did something that upset her. "Please call me back!" I cried. "I am getting anxious!"

She never returned my call.

I kept telling myself that I knew she never loved me, and that I should never have trusted her or allowed her in on any level. I just couldn't wrap my head around the possibility of her loving me at all with how she treated me. I was in shutdown mode because she was ignoring me completely, cutting me off. Telling myself that she never loved me in the first place was black and white thinking as a result of years of her emotional abuse; a coping mechanism to try to keep me safe. It was only useful, if at all, during my childhood. As an adult, it took years to rewire this type of thinking. I didn't have the emotional tools to understand how my mother could have loved me. Her actions were all I knew; all I understood.

When our son Nicholas was born two years later, I sent my mother a baby announcement, and, to my surprise, she called me. But, predictably, we argued.

"Why did you ignore my calls?" I asked her over and over again. "How could you do that, didn't you hear me crying on your answering machine, begging you to call me back? I was crying when I called you from my honeymoon. Didn't it occur to you to call me back?"

Her reply was the same as the many other times I had asked her why she treated me so poorly; it was about her, not me. "You treated me like shit on your wedding day, so I left."

"Mom, I treated you like shit?" I asked her. "It was my day, and the focus was supposed to be on me and Ari," I said as I exhaled loudly. "I really don't understand why you couldn't simply handle being with Christy and Dad that day. I didn't ask for you guys to get divorced. That was your choice. I did what I could to include all three of you on my wedding day. I am sorry that you felt like that was treating you like shit, but it is really the other way around!" I was almost yelling at this point.

That night, we talked for almost two hours as I released pent-up tears. I tried to get answers to questions that were hard to ask. How do you come out and ask your mother why she was so mean to you, or if she ever really wanted you? I brought up the past, those nights when she came home drunk and woke me up at midnight on a school night to clean up cookie crumbs from the kitchen counter. I told her that she hurt my feelings. I told her that when she didn't come home at all, I was scared.

"Mom, our relationship is broken. Normal parents don't stop talking to their teenage children for months. Remember how you ignored me for months when we argued when I was in high school?"

But my words and sobs fell on deaf ears. Her reply was gut punching and emotionless.

"You were a very difficult child to raise, Ashley. I hope that none of your children are so difficult."

I told her to fuck off, and then I hung up. I had to admit that I was never going to have the love of my mother. She was gone, yet I never really had her to begin with.

For months after that call with my mother, I cried at unexpected and awkward moments. I just couldn't get it together. I was torn up. I was a new mother myself, and all I wanted was to be able to call mine and ask questions like "How do I get him to sleep?" and "When do I feed him real food?" You know, have a regular relationship like my friends did with their mothers.

I was desperate to be able to connect with her on any level, and there were parts of her that I did still like. I would have taken her advice on things like baby food and sleep schedules. But my mother chose everything else over me. I felt so lost, hurt, and ugly. I spent months in therapy talking through my grief over the loss of my mother. In my mind, my mother was dead and banished, but in my heart, I was deeply hurt from her abandonment. That hole accumulated fragments of my life.

Like the cupholder in your car, no matter how many times you clean it, you can still see crumbs and lint in the tiny crevasses.

Nicholas was diagnosed with cancer five months after that dreadful call. In the hospital, I asked my father to do me a favor: Make sure no one told my mother that Nicholas was sick. I told him that I couldn't bear for her to be a part of my life. I thought that if she knew, she would make Nicholas's diagnosis, illness, and treatment about her. My dad did as I asked. He kept me safe, as he always had. My mother didn't know.

We were in crisis mode, and my body was in constant fight or flight. The thought of adding the unpredictability of my mother to the mix was too much. My biggest fear was that if she did find out that Nicholas was sick, she would still choose to not show up. That was definitely in the realm of possibilities. I now think that part of me shut her out as a way to protect myself from my biggest fear—her not choosing me or showing up to love me.

I was riddled with anxiety for most of my 30s and 40s. I couldn't really tell you what I was anxious about, and when asked, I would gravitate toward the low-hanging fruit: current world problems, my kids, work, or the pandemic. The reality is that the anxiety that was bouncing around in my body for years was the same anxiety that started when I was little. It was stuck in there because I had not begun to let it out. Every emotion and trigger I deal with to this very day, I can trace back to an adverse event that took place when I was younger.

My childhood was about survival; there was no time nor an invitation to tend to the little girl who felt panicked, lost, angry, hopeless, and heartbroken. I was completely unable to even grasp her basic need to feel accepted, loved, safe, known, or seen. Our feelings are always driven by our needs, and my basic needs were not met as a child. Thus, I spent my life trying to find people and circumstances in which they could be met.

Seeking out circumstances in life and relationships to fill needs and fix emotions is a vicious cycle, because unless we know what the unmet need is we are trying to fill, we think we are trying to heal or fix an emotion. The emotion of feeling self-conscious, for instance, isn't always about looks or driven by success vs failure. Self-conscious could very well be driven by the unmet need for trust, which is ultimately about connection. Until we can establish safety and trust, the feelings of self-conscious cannot be healed.

I thought if I was thin and pretty, I would be loveable. If I worked hard, people would pay attention to me; I would be seen, be heard, feel loved, and on and on. I was searching to fill these holes, but I always came up empty.

Chapter 9
Nicholas

The kind of cancer that Nicholas had was rare all around. It was rare that he was an infant and had cancer, and it was also rare that he had Acute Myelogenous Leukemia (AML). Most childhood leukemias are ALL (Acute Lymphoblastic Leukemia). The genetic makeup of his cancer was only seen in 55-year-old women, and they were all dying from it. The doctors gave us a 50/50 shot that he would survive six months after he finished treatment.

In the dark evenings in our small hospital room, I would pray when I couldn't sleep… which was often. I would stare at the white ceiling tiles and pray to God, asking him to take Nicholas's cancer and give it to me. "Please God, let him make it to kindergarten. Please let him be able to be a little boy even for a while." I just wanted to be able to take him home, even if it was only for a few years, and I was desperate to take away the pain of my helpless 7-month-old son. For 188 straight days, we barely slept between Nicholas being so critical, the nurses coming in every hour to change his medications, and the constant hum of hospital life.

One thing Nicholas did with his tiny little body from 7 months old all the way up to his first birthday was fight. He defied the odds and escaped most everything they told us would happen. The fact that he was still alive after having coded twice was a miracle all by itself. He clung to me or Ari all day and night while he fought his cancer. We held him, kissed him, sang to him, read him books, and gave him baths in a plastic tub on the floor of a hospital room shower.

It was our love for Nicholas that gave him strength; our love and God's love for him that helped him to persevere. Whenever Nicholas could, he would muster a smile, bopping his head along to the Baby Einstein music we played for him. All along the way, he was telling us, "I am going to be OK, Mom and Dad."

While Nicholas was in treatment, my husband did what he does best: analyze data. Ari created fever charts in Excel so that on rounds with our medical team we could discuss the data and make educated guesses as to how Nicholas was responding to treatment, and if his body was trying to tell us something was wrong. Fevers during chemotherapy treatment can be expected, but they can also point to a source of unknown infection.

Ari also took the lead in finding second, third, and fourth opinions for our son. If Ari had not sought opinions of other leading hospitals, we would never have found St. Jude's cutting-edge transplant, The Natural Killer Transplant. Dr. Rubnitz, the head AML doctor at St. Jude, mentioned this transplant to us over a conference call that Ari and I took while sitting in a nearby apartment donated to us by the Greek Church. Years later, I would sit in that same apartment with my brother and sister-in-law while their daughter was also in the hospital.

To take part in the Natural Killer Transplant, Nicholas would need to finish his current regimen, and either Ari or I would need to qualify to be the donor. The procedure took natural killer cells (NK) found among white blood cells from either Mom or Dad, washed them, and then transplanted them into the patient. The intent was that the NK cells would find any cancer cells within the patient, designate them as foreign, and kill them.

I was Nicholas's match.

We flew to Memphis, Tennessee, a few days after Christmas 2007. We rented a nearby apartment and drove Nicholas to St. Jude's daily for treatments, exams, and bloodwork. The chemo regimen that Nicholas needed for this transplant was light in comparison to what he had just finished at Boston Children's Hospital. The doctors just needed to make a little room within his bone marrow for my cells; they didn't need to wipe it clean as they did with his other chemo protocol.

They harvested my NK cells the day before Nicholas's transplant. It was rather easy and painless for me, and although it took several hours, it was a breeze. The machine took out all of my blood, while simultaneously giving me back my red cells. The harvest was for my white cells because that is where the NK cells live.

Nicholas tolerated his transplant well. He drank a bottle of milk and watched his beloved Baby Einstein videos while the doctor pushed over 100 billion of my NK cells through an IV into Nicholas's blood. A few days later, my cells began engrafting into Nicholas's bone marrow. They were doing exactly what we had planned. For a few weeks after his transplant, Nicholas only needed to go to the hospital to get blood draws because they wanted to see if they could see my cells floating around in his circulatory system. As soon as they could no longer see my cells, we left to come home.

We will never know if that is what cured Nicholas or not. What we do know is that he went from 50/50 odds he would survive 6 months to turning 15 the year I wrote this book, in 2021.

My belief? God's plan, my cells, his work.

People had made Nicholas blankets, shirts, bibs, and they brought him toys galore while he was hospitalized. But, I didn't want a single item from the hospital to be brought home. I wanted home to be home, not filled with hospital items. I threw it all out except the religious items from the church. I was desperate for a fresh start.

In order to go home, Nicholas had to see the dentist and eye doctor. The hospital rooms are on the opposite side of the hospital from the outpatient clinics, where he would get his discharge exams. Ari was making trips home with our clothes and personal items while I brought Nicholas to the eye doctor. I had him in his stroller and I dressed him in real clothes (rather than a onesie as I had for the last six months).

As I stood in the elevator going up to the eye clinic, it hit me. It had been six straight months of living here, and I had not put him in his stroller like that since he was 7 months old. Surrounded by strangers, I began to cry. It didn't even occur to me to wipe my tears. I just let them roll down my face until the BING of the elevator sounded. That sound was my alarm to push aside the strong emotions that were coming up, and get the job done so we could go home. No time to feel sorry for ourselves. No time to feel.

That is exactly what I did. Pushed aside my sadness. I didn't think about the grief I was feeling for losing that six months in regular people life with our little boy. What I most certainly didn't feel was the fear that was building up inside me as I faced my new normal. I told myself to be grateful he was alive and enjoy the time we have with him, and to not look back.

Don't look back; it is bad back there.

We drove home like brand-new parents, Ari checking in on him while I drove. Nicholas slept the entire ride. But home was not what I had dreamt of all those nights in the hospital. Our house smelled stale, stuffy, and weird. We put our things down and looked at each other, not knowing what to do next. For most of the following year, Nicholas couldn't be out of sight without having terrible separation anxiety. He had a difficult time sleeping, and it didn't help that we were weaning him off his methadone. Yes, they give high-dose opiates to all cancer patients, even infants. He was withdrawing from his pain meds, in a new environment, and we all needed sleep. It took us months before we found our new rhythm.

The day he started pre-kindergarten, almost a year later, I cried for the entire two and a half hours he was in school. I had not been without him in so long that my arms felt empty. I lay in bed and worried. Was he missing me? Was he OK without me? Was he scared? Did he want me to come and get him?

I had been protecting and advocating for him day and night for almost a year and a half at this point, and I was lost without him by my side. I told the doctors and nurses what to do, and I watched Nicholas like a hawk. He was our everything; our only focus.

That day, all I did was lay in bed crying and waiting for the clock to turn 11:45, signaling that it was time to leave for pick up. I tried to hide my puffy eyes so the teacher didn't think I was a lunatic. I opened the door to his classroom, scanning feverishly looking for Nicholas. I was so worried I was going to find him crying in the teacher's arms. But there he was, playing in the sandbox and smiling with his new buddy.

I started crying all over again. My heart was so full. He was a regular little boy, just as I had been praying for such a long time. He was playing! *He was playing!* His eyes found mine, and he ran right into my arms. We were together again. My Nicholas. My sweet, sweet boy. I loved him so much in that moment. He took my hand, I grabbed his backpack, and we went home.

Nicholas beat the odds. He is a thriving and healthy young man today. He continues to persevere in everything he does. Our son is an old soul, sent here to earth for the greater good of everyone he meets. I certainly know he was given to me for my greater good. I love you Nicholas.

———————

For years, I was stuck in the weeds, not knowing that there was a bigger picture. 20/20 is easy in hindsight, but I must have missed school the day they handed out those glasses! I certainly learned the hard way, but today, I believe I have more than one life purpose.

Here is my 10,000-foot view.

I found Ari, and he gave me the unconditional love I had only received from my father up to that point in my life. Ari gave me the wings to fly; his love gave me power. Without my husband's love, I would likely have been living a life full of suffering without much hope for healing. Together, we created Nicholas. Nicholas gets cancer, and I am the genetic match he needs for a rare treatment. Without Nicholas having cancer, I would never have started a charity that has helped over 13,000 families also get through their journey with pediatric cancer. If Nicholas had not had cancer, I would never have been able to be as present for my brother and sister-in-law when their daughter Evi was sick.

In the middle of all this, I found Reiki at a dark time in my life. If I had not, I would never have become a Reiki therapist or meditation teacher as well, helping so many people through their own dark times. Every single awful and difficult time in my life has been for a reason.

When you think about it, dharma is *deep*, man!

Chapter 10
The Helper

When people need me, I go. Oftentimes, I am already on the way when they call. I will drop everything to help people that I love. Everything. As an example, when my niece Evi was in the hospital, I gave up my youngest daughter's first year of life so I could be there for Evi's parents, BJ and Tiffany. I spent almost every day, excluding weekends, in the hospital with them. I had no idea what this was doing to my body, and I wouldn't have cared even if someone *had* told me. I would have said, "But they need me, and Evi needs me. I have to go in and sit with them. If I am able to, I need to go."

From the moment I first met BJ, we became fast friends. BJ is larger than life, has a contagious smile, and everyone wants to be friends with him. When BJ brings you into his inner circle, you feel special. He shaves his head bald and wears a t-shirt and shorts even in the dead of winter; he is just simple like that, which makes him easy to be around. When he walks into a room, he captivates everyone in it.

My husband's family is Greek—from "the mountains" in Greece, to be exact. They all have big hands and strong features, and BJ is no exception. My sister-in-law Tiffany is a quiet, dainty and petite blonde. Her acquiescent and introspective personality is overpowered by her loud and strong-willed husband. Tiffany loves fashion and wears the classic styles of Chanel and

Gucci better than any woman I know. BJ, Tiffany, and I will always share a special bond. What I bore witness to alongside them will forever have a place in my heart.

My body had already been through the nightmare of living in the hospital—the sleepless nights, not eating, the chaos of doctor meetings, the stress and worry—when Nicholas had leukemia in 2006. Now, I was doing it again, living on adrenaline for Evi; for BJ and Tiffany. I was running on autopilot, back in fight-or-flight before I had even recovered from Nicholas being sick.

I was with them in the hospital from the day after Evi was born on Cape Cod. They transferred her to Boston Children's so she could receive state of the art care. Evi was living in the very hospital that cared for her cousin Nicholas four years earlier.

Upon my arrival, I had a deep-down dark feeling that I was going to be coming back to that place often. There was a part of me that felt comfortable being back in the hospital; comfortable because I had just lived there for months, and comfortable because my brain was wired for crisis. I found Tiffany in a nursing room, pumping milk into her breast pump. We sat and talked while those tiny little pumps made that squeaking noise. I asked Tiffany for an update, to tell me what she knew so far. She told me that Evi needed heart and bowel surgery, and then she started to cry.

"I know from BJ that Nicholas was sick when he was a baby too, and I have heard you speak at One Mission events, but I can't do that. I don't know how to be that mom; I am not strong enough. I can't do this."

I sat down right in front of her and said, "You are already doing it, Tiff. You *are* strong enough to do this. I felt the same way you feel right now; you are not alone."

I felt the feelings of desperation behind her lament because I knew she didn't want this life. She didn't want to have a critically ill baby, and she certainly didn't want what was coming down the pipeline. None of us did.

I felt the same way when my son was diagnosed. All you think is *NO, NO, NO—this isn't happening,* and *I don't want to do this.* As if saying it out loud will make your plea heard or make it all stop. You pray to The Big Guy, "Hear me, hear my desperate prayers for help." But when confronted with a situation like this, you have to handle it. There is no choice.

In an honest attempt to calm her, I told Tiffany, "You don't have a choice. Each day, you will get up and handle what the day brings you. You can do this. I will be here with you, and I'll do my best to help where I can." As if the Universe knew we needed a comic interlude, the breast pump squeaked. We needed the laugh!

For the next 16 months, I was in and out of that hospital on the regular. Many days, I worked on One Mission-related items from Evi's window seat. I was lucky to have a great team working for me at the time, and working from her hospital room or the cafeteria on breaks worked out well.

Tiffany and I sang songs to her with the music therapist, played healing music, and read books to her. I ran errands for BJ and Tiffany, and I set them up in a nearby apartment so their son Byron, who was being watched by Tiffany's mother, could be close to them during those long, dark days. I took Byron for them overnight to give them a break so they could sleep. I did their Christmas shopping.

You name it—if they needed it, I jumped to do it.

Though most of the time BJ, Tiffany and I sat by Evi's bed in her tiny ICU room and talked over and over about the details of her medical decisions. I didn't have any answers, so I just listened and did my best to contribute when possible.

Evi eventually had her heart surgery and was recovering well. Her bowels had been moved to the correct location, and her medical team was pleased with her progress. Something was still wrong with our girl though; she was passing out almost every time she breast-fed. After months of exploration, her surgeon figured out that there was a part of her anatomy that was crushing her trachea. She literally couldn't breathe.

Her last and final surgery was to open and fix her airway so she could breathe normally again. Boston Children's had never done a surgery like this before, and at the time, Evi was only the fifth child in the country to have airway surgery within the first month of life.

The surgery of her airway left her with a lot of scar tissue, and just like when you get a cut your scab flakes off, Evi's did too. Except when her scabs sloughed off, they plugged her airway, and she would stop breathing. When this would happen, Evi would go into cardiac arrest, which happened often as her body was trying to heal itself. The days and nights were getting very intense with worry for all of us, but mostly for BJ and Tiffany.

I felt helpless—all I could do was sit and hold space for them. I couldn't fix Evi, and I couldn't take away the pain they were experiencing as her parents. Helplessness has to be one of the most troublesome emotions a person combats in life, and for an empath, it is even heavier.

The brains of those who have experienced trauma are wired to avoid pain. That is what the excess worrying is for—trying to plan accordingly in order to avoid future pain. I had been living this way since I was little, always looking around to ensure the house was tidy before my mother came home and replaying possible scenarios of her anger at me—all in preparation for what could possibly happen. If I prepared myself for the worst, I reasoned that when it happened it would hurt less; be less of a shock.

There are times in my life that I still do this today. It will happen out of nowhere, and all of a sudden, I will just start thinking and replaying a horrible scenario of either my husband or children getting sick, a bad car accident, or other terrible scenarios. My brain will just take off, fabricating a story and thinking it is in control.

Here's the thing: Our brains know what we teach them. My anxiety, childhood neglect, and emotional abuse had taught my brain to be anxious and to think bad thoughts. I had to take control and re-teach my brain; something I ultimately did down the road.

From the time I got my driver's license, I always loved to drive. It made me feel in control, and that made me feel safe. When I got married, I was striving to be the perfect wife and a smart businesswoman, both designed to keep Ari loving me because having his love made me feel safe. When I walked into a party, I quickly assessed everyone in the room, sizing up the guests; all designed to ensure my safety. After Nicholas battled cancer, I began to obsess about medical issues for me, Ari and our children; all to ensure that none of us would ever come down with something as awful as cancer again. I was in a constant state of low-level hypervigilance. This anxiety, this hypervigilance alone would have taken me months or years in therapy to unravel and heal, and I was not in therapy. Rather, all of that anxiety kept piling up in every cell of my body.

The person who showed up to help BJ and Tiffany was broken in every way. I was broken, carrying around so much anxiety from my childhood and

Nicholas's cancer. I was on empty every morning I left the house to go to the hospital. I was an engine whose oil had not been replaced or changed in years. Like the car, I was still running but not efficiently, and eventually, the engine would seize. Evi was critically ill and I was feeling helpless. Helplessness and hypervigilance are like gasoline and fire. Feelings of helplessness come from trauma. Think about it: we literally were once trapped and could not help ourselves. Hypervigilance, on the other hand, is a mechanism of trying to get safe. Each day I was in that hospital, it was sending my nervous system signals that I was trapped and not safe. Yet I kept looking for safety. It was an automatic cycle that kept going and going. All the while, my oil was getting dirtier and dirtier. Soon enough, my engine was going to seize.

It was instinctual for me to hold onto my emotions, and now I was holding onto BJ and Tiffany's too. Empaths do this often—we think that in order to show up and be a good helper, we must hold onto the emotions of those we are helping. It is our automatic, default setting to show up, give everything, and absorb every ounce of pain from those around us.

Evi, BJ, and Tiffany were all I ever talked about. When people asked me how I was doing, I would give them her current medical status, and it was usually very grim. I told her story to so many people, I felt like I had nothing else to talk about, nothing else that was important. I felt guilty when I wasn't with them, and I lived with a very morose attitude, almost as if I was in mourning with them. I felt like it was the right thing to do, to be sad because my family was sad. And my brain and body got the message loud and clear: *We are in crisis.*

My thoughts were telling my body to hunker down and prepare. This meant that I was not sleeping or digesting my food, my heart rate was always too high, and I was generally unwell. My brain knew this crisis state thoroughly. What it didn't know how to do was to be present, happy, or calm.

At the time, I didn't understand how to show up for someone without my entire being living in their pain. I took on other people's crises like they were my emergency. In fact, this was how I showed up—how I was a "good friend." Open up and drink it all down. I didn't know how to slow down, assess the true emergency, and take care of myself before stepping into the lives of those I wanted to help. I just didn't know how to not give my all.

Chapter 11
Wipers

There are so many memories etched into my brain from our time in the hospital with Evi. She had been there for almost a year, and had countless surgeries trying to open up her airway. But the day that my brother-in-law BJ called me from the Cape while he was checking on their house and collecting mail makes me cry even when I think about today. I can still hear his cry: "ASHLEY.... ASHLEY!"

"Yes, BJ, what is it? What's wrong?"

"The baby coded," he said. "I am two hours away; I won't make it in time. Can you get there? CAN YOU GET TO THEM?!" He was panicking.

"Yes, I can get to them. I am on my way."

I hung up and called our nanny, Alaina. I told her I needed her and asked her to leave school. She was 15 minutes away at Mass Bay Community College. I left my napping child, Zoe, in her crib alone and headed out on the highway to Boston, a 40-minute drive without traffic. I prayed the entire drive that Alaina would get there before Zoe woke up. Suddenly, feelings of guilt washed over me.

What if the house caught fire? What if Zoe climbed out of her crib and hurt herself? What kind of a mother leaves her child sleeping alone in a house?

I drove 100 mph down the Mass Pike with my hazard lights AND my windshield wipers on, even though it wasn't raining. I have no idea why I put the wipers on. Maybe I was thinking the unusual movement would scare everyone out of the way and they would move over for me. And, of course, the ONE time you want to get pulled over, the cops were nowhere in sight. If they stopped me, I would get a police escort to the hospital, blowing through traffic with lights and sirens. Instead, I drove my little Porsche convertible at 100 mph, barely feeling the speed.

I pulled into the valet area at Boston Children's Hospital way too fast, and all the valet guys looked at me like they were going to yell at me for my reckless driving:

"Ma'am… Oh hi," one of the regulars said, recognizing me as soon as he looked up. I threw him the key and screamed, "I HAVE TO GET INSIDE! SHE CODED!"

As I ran into the crowded lobby of the hospital, I knew that I didn't have time to wait for the elevators. So, I took the stairs. How I knew where the staircase was, I have no idea. I ran up all eight flights. I swung the door open onto the 8th floor and frantically pressed the button to be buzzed in.

"IT'S ASHLEY, IS SHE ALIVE?! Tell me she is ALIVE!" They buzzed me in, and I fell over the top of the front desk, sweating and panting.

"She is alive," the front desk lady said between my bated breaths. "But you can't go back right now, they are trying to stabilize her."

So, I waited for what seemed like at least an hour. They eventually let me back, which I can't believe they did. The hospital staff just bent the rules for us: me, my husband Ari, and BJ and Tiffany, too.

Ari and BJ are best friends. They talk several times a day. During the time Evi was in the hospital, my husband ran his family's business that was started by their grandparents, Cumberland Farms, a convenience store chain up and down the East Coast with a few sites in Florida. The four of us treated our medical teams like family, and that could be the reason they bent the rules for us. We got personal with them, and they did with us as well. Nicholas was one of the sickest kids on the oncology floor, just as was Evi on the cardiac floor. I think the nurses and doctors felt badly for us, so they let us do things that others were not allowed to.

I walked into Evi's room and was immediately pushed back against the wall. The doctors were still working on her, and there was blood everywhere. I mean everywhere—all over the floor, the walls, the ceiling. I scanned the room and saw Tiffany standing at the foot of Evi's bed, stunned and clutching her thin gold necklace.

I walked over to her and tried to hold her up, but she fell back into my arms while we watched the doctors try to save her daughter. She was grasping her necklace so tightly that she eventually snapped it off her neck.

Orders were being called out by the head doctor, and nurses were scrambling trying to keep up with what he needed to save Evi. At one point, someone came in and took us out. About a half an hour later, one by one, Evi's nurses came out of the unit doors. They all had tears in their eyes, visibly exhausted and defeated. Stephanie was the one I was closest to, and I still chat with her today from time to time. She walked right into my arms. She needed a hug, and she needed to cry! "She is alive, but barely," she whispered in my ear.

Everything happened so fast. They took Evi to the operating room, and I waited with Tiffany for our husbands to arrive. It was close to 3 p.m. when I realized Tiffany had not eaten anything all day. Her usual schedule was to arrive at the hospital around 7 a.m. and stay until 7 p.m. after the night shift arrived. That day was no different, but Tiffany had not had a morsel of food. Her usual size two pants were falling off her. My goal was to get her some orange juice because she needed the sugar, so we went back into Evi's room to grab our bags.

Her bed was gone, and the room felt so empty, so big without it. Emergency equipment was everywhere—syringes, bloody gauze, white rolls of half-used medical tape, papers, tubing—just an incredible overflow of hospital debris. We stood there taking it all in and Tiffany finally cried. She was shaking, and my body was on fire. I was steady on the outside, but on the inside, my organs were shaking. It felt like I had birds flying around in all parts of my body, like a fluttering happening all over but on the inside.

You can't un-see the blood of your baby niece splattered all around the floor and walls of her hospital room. It is impossible for me to forget the vision: the pictures my own children had made for their cousin hanging on the walls of her barren bed space, amongst the life-saving equipment the hospital staff left behind. It was a sobering, horrifying scene.

I was worried that by the time BJ got to the hospital, Evi would be gone. I called Ari and told him he needed to come to the hospital to sit with us while Evi was in surgery. They needed to stop her bleeding, and they had every doctor on her team in the OR. I called Alaina and told her I had no idea when I was going to be home. That became my usual call: always asking her to stay late or come in on her days off. Even to this day, almost 11 years later, my daughter Zoe will ask me something about her childhood, or when she was a baby, and my response will be, "I don't know; that was when Alaina raised you."

All of Zoe's baby pictures were on Alaina's phone. She potty trained her, she took her to playdates, she sang her songs. I missed almost all of Zoe's first year. There is a part of me that holds guilt about this, and at the same time, I believe I was exactly where God wanted me to be: with Evi, helping her parents in any way I could.

Evi survived this episode, but she would have more. Her little body was getting tired. The many cardiac episodes had been depriving her brain of oxygen; each episode lasting for over five minutes or longer. Her doctors were fearing that her brain function would be severely hindered. There were so many times I would drive home from visiting them in complete silence—no radio, no talking on the phone. I was frozen in shock. In fact, I would ignore all incoming calls. My body was frozen in the war zone that was almost every day in that cardiac ICU.

During those months, if we were lucky enough to have Evi stable, we would celebrate with music therapy or take a longer break down in the café. It was the cardiac episode that she had the day after Thanksgiving 2011 that she never recovered from. We were all desperate for a miracle, and we prayed so hard for God to save Evi. It just was not her plan to stay with us on this earth; a plan we all still struggle with today.

Our Evi died on January 2, 2012. She will be forever loved.

When I look back on all of these moments with Evi, Nicholas, and even my mother, it often feels like they happened to someone else rather than me. When you read them on paper, they seem so drastic, so earth shattering… so traumatic. When you are living them, moments like these are just that—*moments* in a life that is full of chaos and heartache. You almost don't even see how it could ever stop, how life will ever be normal again. Yet, it happens. Life carries on, and so do you.

I had two more children after Nicholas, but when we were in the throes of it with him, I vowed never to have more children because I couldn't take the pain of having another sick child. Similarly, when I was little, I vowed never to love anyone because the risk of pain was too great. Then I met Ari.

Life is never constant. I am learning that now—that people change, situations change, and our emotions shift and change. All we need to do is hang on, breathe, and allow the natural flow of life to do what it knows to do: shift and change. The more I lean into this and allow the uncertainty of life to unfold, the happier and freer I feel. My suffering was at its worst when I was trying to hold onto the past, using it to predict my future. I was trying to control and hold onto people, situations, and life. I wanted control because I feared the unknown.

I get it now, that we don't have control of the future. All we can do is be in the present and let the Universe know what we want for our future. But then we need to let the dream float away into the Universe to get cooked up to come back to us. I think my theme song should be "Let It Go," from the movie *Frozen:*

Let it go… Let it go… Can't hold back anymore… Let it go!

I remember my father trying to explain to me years after Nicholas was finished with his cancer treatment how traumatic it was for him to watch Nicholas so sick, and how it was even more difficult for him to see me so distraught. He felt helpless. It was not until I sat with BJ and Tiffany for those 16 months of Evi's life that I finally understood what he meant.

Going through a trauma is easier than watching those you love go through it. When you are in the middle of a crisis like having a sick child, you are in fight or flight mode 24/7. There is no time to think or take inventory of your emotional state. You are in "Do" mode. When you are sitting by and watching a loved one battle a crisis, there is not much *doing* happening. So, you are forced to sit and watch, and you feel helpless.

For a victim of trauma, feeling helpless sets off signals in the nervous system that we are in danger. My body thought I was in danger while I watched BJ and Tiffany suffer, because of the danger I felt when I was helpless as a child being abused. The feeling of helplessness was appropriate for the present moment, but my brain and nervous system could not decipher between my past and the present moment. This inability to see the present moment for what it was became a pattern that repeated for years. My body and brain were responding to the circumstances of others I witnessed around me as if it were happening to me.

Anna once told me this phrase: "Other people's crises do not need to be my chaos." Needless to say, that hit me like a ton of bricks. From that moment on, and still to this day, I remind myself of this important self-care technique every day with a sticky note on my computer.

My deep need to help people when I see they are suffering kicks every cell in my body into high gear, and I get consumed with the situation. I have been this way since I was little. This has not always been a good thing for me or the people that I "help." For one, people need to *want* help, and if you try to force help on them, it can ruin relationships. Also, you can't truly help people if you are not also helping yourself at the same time. Lastly, you must never put your own family aside to help others. This will backfire. I know it did for me.

I can't tell you how many arguments I have had with my husband where my grandiose and deep need to help others comes up as a sticking point for him. He would ask me over and over again, "Why do you feel the need to help all of these people? Why are you ignoring us in order to help the world?" Recently, he asked me point blank if I was trying to be a hero. I was stunned, but scared at the same time. I felt like he didn't even know me.

Then I asked myself, "Why do I do this? Why do I get so consumed with making sure people who need my help get it?" Perhaps they weren't such outlandish questions after all.

This is just another reason why Ari is the perfect partner for me—he asks the tough questions, and together we go deep into our emotional states to make changes, both as individuals and as a couple. Oftentimes this begins with an argument, but hey, nobody's perfect!

So, I pondered, journaled, and, of course, talked with my therapist about this deep need. "Why do I help all these people, oftentimes at my own expense?" I asked Anna one session.

"Let's ask this question, Ashley," Anna replied softly. "First, does what Ari said resonate with you? Do you go above and beyond to help people who you see are in need?"

I replied quickly and emphatically. "Yes, I do this."

"OK. Now let's take a breather break and check in with your body right now," Anna guided me.

I closed my eyes, and let each part of my body relax, bit by bit, from my eyelids to my feet.

"Why do you help people so deeply and wholeheartedly, Ashley?" she asked. I took a deep breath and began to cry.

"I see there are emotions coming up," she said. "Can you tell me about them?"

"I just can't walk away when I see someone suffering. I don't want them to feel alone," I said as I continued crying. "I just don't want them to feel like I don't love them or that they are not loved at all."

"Why?" Anna asked.

"Because I know what it feels like to be scared, alone, and hurting, and nobody came to help me. Nobody helped me." I was sobbing at this point. "I can't watch someone suffer and leave them alone; I didn't want to be left alone. I wanted someone to help me, and I needed someone to love me. I wanted to be rescued. I can't ever rest knowing that someone needed help and for them to think I passed them by. I want to rescue them, and I will stop at nothing to bring them to safety. I can't rest until I rescue them." It took a few moments to calm down and for Anna to begin talking again. She was letting me have my moment.

"I see that, Ashley. I can see you have a big heart and care deeply about those you love. Would it be OK if we talked about what is happening in your nervous system during these situations? It may help you to better answer the question of why you help."

"Of course," I answered.

"When you see people suffering, their suffering is a trigger for you. Your brain and nervous system go back into fight or flight mode easily and quickly because it doesn't see that it is someone else that is in pain, rather than you. Your body is responding as if you are the victim here, and not your loved one. It is important that you recognize this first and foremost—that your body thinks it is back in your childhood home, or in the hospital with Nicholas or Evi. Your body is in a trauma response and will do everything and anything to fix the problem because it wants to feel safe again. It is their situation of being unsafe that is making you feel unsafe; but it is not your truth."

I was hanging on her every word. "Second," she continued, "the years of neglect that you endured have given you the ability to empathize with people who you see as alone. Yes, it is a gift to be able to see suffering in others and to offer help. But part of your work and part of how you take care of yourself is to offer the help, and then give people space to help themselves. You can't fix people's lives for them, just like nobody can fix yours for you. We must all be an active participant in our own healing.

"To recap, first, I want you to see when you are triggered. I want you to notice that when you are a witness to other people's suffering, your body goes into fight or flight. If you can see it, you can do the work that needs to happen to calm your body down. When you are calm, you can offer help. It is up to them if they take it. Regardless, you and your body need to remember that you are safe. You are safe. "

This session with Anna was likely one of my most meaningful. She gave me a gift in this session—she unburdened me. I not only clearly understood that I was getting re-triggered each time I saw someone in need of a rescue, but that I actually couldn't heal anyone other than me. Her words sat in my bones for days, and I felt lighter and more at peace than I had felt in years, when thinking about those who I loved who were in pain.

We all have to do our own healing. It is not my job to swoop in and save anyone. As adults, we must embark on our own healing journey, and unfortunately, some never do.

When I see people around me suffering, sick, or needing help, my nervous system kicks in and I become consumed with helping them. I help because I care, yes, but I get consumed *because of my trauma.*

When you help others, do you have boundaries? Do you make sure that you are healthy, grounded, and feeling full before you put everything on the line to help others? Or are you like me, coming from a place of trauma and trying to help others at your own expense?

I spent years of my life putting others first;
I was trying to save them because nobody came to save me.
I was living in the past. Are you?

Chapter 12
A Pool of Hurt

A few weeks after Evi's funeral, I found myself in the emergency room because I thought I had appendicitis. A few months after that, I popped a rib at the gym. I was in and out of the doctor's office with urinary symptoms, abdominal pain, headaches, and dizziness—the list goes on.

I'd lost my trust in my own body and faith that there was still good in the world. I was convinced that I was going to be the next one to have something bad happen to them. So, when any physical symptom popped up, I believed it was my body telling me that something was wrong. I wish that my doctor could have seen through all of it, because the tests always came back fine. What would my life have been like if she sat me down and told me my anxiety and PTSD caused my illnesses? Maybe she didn't know it herself.

What the doctor *did* see was that I was a zombie. The response was always the same: "You need to lower your stress level." I worked 12-hour days, dealt with the kids at night after the nanny left, and then I slept. A lot. I worked and took naps during the day if I didn't have meetings, I was dizzy all the time, and I cried a lot. But somehow, some way, I always appeared well enough on the outside that people thought I was fine.

I'd worked so hard helping BJ and Tiffany through arguments, doctor's appointments, and being emotionally available to them, but I was barely through my own grief from Nicholas's journey. It was just the tipping point my body needed to start the crumble. I did what I could to appear normal in the aftermath of losing Evi, but after she died, I started to fall apart. After those months in the hospital with her, I simply started my crash and burn.

I was depleted, living in a pool of hurt, and thought I had nothing left to give. I found myself feeling alone, stranded, scared, and being sick. I was fully aware that I was living every day in fear, but I had no idea how to make it stop. I was ready; I just didn't have any tools. I knew it was time for me to heal. I made the decision that I would do anything to feel better, to put myself back together. And, as The Universe had so many times before, it brought me a path to healing. The Universe brought me Lucinda.

When we go through a trauma (or witness a trauma), there is a jolt of energy that infiltrates our nervous system. It sends a shockwave into our bodies, and if sustained for too long, our bodies can't find the way back to baseline without an intervention. After those months with Nicholas's treatment, I needed help getting my nervous system back in check. However, I stopped therapy too soon, and I used work as a numbing mechanism. Meanwhile, the trauma was stuck inside my body, and every little disturbance I experienced after Nicholas retraumatized me all over again.

At that point, I'd run as fast as I could for 22 years, trying to help anyone I could. I was the one who people called when they needed a good doctor referral for their sick child. I was the one who dropped everything when people needed me. I spent years helping others at my own expense, constantly looking outward. "Who can I help and what more can I accomplish in life?" was my motto. Meanwhile, what lived on the inside of me was starving for attention. I was running hard. However, the reality was I was running *from* something, not *to* something.

Humans are a complex system: mind, ego, body, and spirit. The human brain experiences pain and suffering only once before it knows it never wants to experience the same pain again.

Let's say you are walking in the forest and step on a sharp, rusty nail, get an infection, and end up in the hospital. Rare, but possible. Now, the next time you get invited for a hike in the woods, your brain thinks hiking equals walking in the woods equals nail, pain, hospital... NOPE.

So, in order to warn and protect you, your brain anticipates a hospital stay and begins experiencing anxiety or pain as it tries to protect you from stepping on yet another nail.

I was five years old when my anxiety began trying to protect me. To this day, the song "Jump" by Van Halen will bring me back to waiting for the school bus with a terrified feeling in my stomach. I experienced anxiety daily in the form of stomachaches and headaches, and I would often try to explain to the school nurse how I "just felt weird." My mind was in overdrive because my body was sending it crisis signals while trying to protect me.

In my case, my mind was trying to protect me from my mother.

Chapter 13
Take the Test

I started monthly Reiki sessions with Lucinda in 2011 and continued for almost six months. My body responded well to her treatments. I was feeling less anxious, and my body hurt less. I would count down the days until I could get on her table again. Lucinda gave healing sessions in her basement, which had the most magical big picture window that overlooked her backyard. The lighting was perfect. She placed a few large selenite crystals on the windowsill, and as they are designed to, I could feel them clearing my energy every time my feet would line up in their path.

Her hands were magic. Each session started off the same way. Lucinda would say a prayer before she placed her hands on me. During her prayer, Lucinda asked for the guidance of her guides, my guides, and her Reiki masters, and also included any questions I had posed to her about my healing path. Upon finishing the prayer, she would place her hands on my shoulders, and we would settle into each other's energy. This was my favorite moment— when she first put her hands on me. I felt cared for, and my body would relax on such a deep level. It was as if my body took an energetic breath.

As I was leaving Lucinda's house one day, after another amazing Reiki session, I asked her what she had planned for the weekend. She told me that she was teaching a Reiki class, and right away I knew that I wanted to become her student. The decision was made without checking my calendar... even though I'd be spending an entire weekend with her, away from my family, learning how to heal myself and others! I knew the opportunity was just what I had been waiting for. I was ready to take my own healing to the next level. While the list of maladies that I had been dealing with since 2006 was not as long (or severe) as it had been before I started seeing Lucinda, I was still dealing with too many physical issues to ignore.

There were many times I would sit with Lucinda before one of our sessions and tell her I knew something was wrong with me. I wanted her to use her psychic powers to figure it out. Unfortunately, it never worked quite like that. What Reiki *did* help me with was to get in tune with my own body, and ultimately, I was able to advocate for myself and ask for the right medical tests. I had recently found a new doctor, one who specialized in Functional Medicine, and while I was driving to the appointment, I listened to some of my calming meditation music as I prayed for answers.

"Please help me find out what is wrong with my body. Dear God, please help me," I prayed. As I wiped tears from my face, I heard a low bellowing voice in my car say the words "LYME TEST."

I screamed out loud. "HELLO?!"

Great, now I am hearing things! I brushed this whole moment off as I walked into the appointment and forgot about the words I heard in the car. I focused on answering the new doctor's rapid-fire questions.

Do you wake up in the middle of the night? What time?
How do you feel first thing in the morning?
Do you still get your period? Is it regular?

All were questions that none of my other doctors ever asked me. Functional Medicine, as defined by The Institute of Functional Medicine is: "Medicine [that] determines how and why illness occurs and restores health by addressing the root causes of disease for each individual."

This process of treating patients is so different than seeing a traditional Western doctor. Making the change to Functional Medicine not only helped me heal from Lyme disease, but it was how I finally uncovered what was truly wrong with me. I continue to see a Functional Medicine doctor today, and I could not imagine any other way to heal my body. It just makes sense to me: going after the root cause rather than throwing a band-aid of medication at a symptom or illness.

After 30 minutes of questions and answers, the doctor ordered a bunch of blood work to be used as a diagnostic point. As I was about to leave, I remembered what I heard in my car. I asked for Lyme disease test, and she gave me *The Look*. You know the one, where people think you are crazy or are annoyed that you are questioning their authority.

"Well, have you been bitten by a tick?" I couldn't remember, but I told her that ticks are all around where I live. Hesitantly, she added the test to the order, and I told her I would pay out of pocket for it. Two weeks later, she called me and told me that not only did I have Lyme disease, but I had chronic Lyme. I'd had the disease for several years, undiagnosed.

I had never been so happy as to finally hear that I was sick, although I didn't want to be sick. I was relieved to find out that how I had been feeling for years wasn't in my head. The dizziness, fatigue, joint pain, abdominal pain—all of it was my body telling me something was wrong.

The high I felt from finally getting a diagnosis didn't last, though. I saw the doctor a week later and found that curing Lyme disease was a black hole of medication and symptom relief. The meds make you feel worse at the beginning stage, which is often called "die-off" or a "herxheimer reaction." My doctor added five new daily antibiotics, in addition to an anti-malarial drug. Every cell in my body was revolting.

I hate taking medication, but Lucinda taught me to give my medication Reiki every day before I took it. Each morning, afternoon, and evening I would lay out my 15 pills on the counter and hold my hands above the pile and give it Reiki just as I would a client. The intent was for my body to accept these medications and help it to eradicate all of the Lyme. This worked… until it didn't.

One day, I was unable to swallow the pills. I physically couldn't get myself to take them, and I knew I had to find another way to rid my body of Lyme. It wasn't that the Reiki stopped working, rather that my body knew the pile of pills was not how I was going to heal this disease.

I finished 14 weeks of the Lyme medication and then called my doctor and told her I was done. I simply couldn't swallow another pill. There was a pull inside of me that kept telling me Reiki was my answer. There I was, picking up the breadcrumbs that The Universe had dropped for me. When presented with a difficult situation, if we look back and see who and what The Universe gave us for breadcrumbs, we can usually find our path to healing.

Oftentimes, we don't know why we bump into old friends, or meet people "for no particular reason," and it is usually months later that it makes sense. Breadcrumbs.

As I looked back, I remember meeting Lucinda at a time when I was so low and sick—when I had Lyme but had not learned of it yet. I thought back to how all those months had gone by with her sessions bringing me back to life bit by bit. The Universe brought me Lucinda when I had Lyme, and I saw that as a sign to use my newfound gift of Reiki to heal the disease I had been seeking to uncover for all these years.

Once my Lyme symptoms began to lift and I was feeling better, I made the decision that my Lyme was gone. I refuse to think about Lyme disease as a part of my life. I know so many others that, after diagnosis, deal with and chase their symptoms of Lyme for their entire life. They go from doctor to doctor, medications to herbs, and so on. I didn't see that as a part of what my life was going to be. It just didn't resonate with me on any level.

It was my belief that I was healed from Lyme that healed me from Lyme. I can see that now, as I heal myself from migraines. Changing my thoughts healed my body. What I couldn't completely figure out was why I could change my thoughts so easily about Lyme, like literally flipping a switch, but when it came to the migraines I experienced four years later in 2019, I was unable to apply the same approach.

Everything is energy—from the events that take place in our lives, to the thoughts we have about those situations, to our emotions and decisions. I believed that if I allowed myself to stay in the dark hole of Lyme disease treatment that I would never get out, because I would be holding onto that energy. The Universe responds to what we think, believe, and feel. If I kept worrying about Lyme disease and constantly thought about my next treatment, I would be staying in the energy of Lyme disease and The Universe would give me back more Lyme disease. So, I turned my back on it, leaving it all behind. It actually seemed easy, this letting go thing.

I struggled with migraines for nearly two years before I began seeing clear relief. So, why was I able to cut the cord so easily with Lyme and not with my chronic pain?

Each of those illnesses had different things to teach me and ways to help me grow. The chronic pain and anxiety was an infinitely larger teacher than the Lyme, and it hung around for as long as needed to help me learn what I, indeed, had come to earth to figure out.

Lyme taught me to listen to my inner voice, and to advocate for myself. The loud bellowing man voice I heard in my car that day was me! I asked for answers and I believed I would get answers, so I did. First, Lyme taught me to trust myself, and then to stand my ground with my doctor. Everyone I know fears the white coat, usually deferring to what the person wearing it provides for a diagnosis and treatment. Not me. Second, Lyme taught me that I had the power to change my life through my thoughts. When we hear the lessons, the dis-ease goes away. I heard the call to listen to my inner voice and stand my ground, and thus my Lyme went away. It served its purpose.

My migraines taught me to sit in what was uncomfortable without the ability or desire to change it. My anxiety taught me to go within to find my peace rather than filling up from the external world. And when the time was right and I was ready, I was able to apply my "I am done approach" to my migraines and anxiety. I threw out my TENS unit (Transcutaneous Electrical Nerve Stimulation), a device used in treatment of my migraines in a goodbye ceremony, cutting the cord and releasing the energy of the sick me. This goodbye ceremony educated my brain that we no longer are sick, and on that day, I began to pave new neural pathways in my brain in regards to migraines.

It took me two years to throw out my TENS unit, but I went from taking it everywhere with me to throwing it in the trash. While my decision to be done with Lyme was much faster than making the decision to throw out my TENS unit, it happened exactly on time in both cases.

My migraines were a much bigger animal than my Lyme, with way more pieces to it that I needed to let go of. The TENS unit was just one part of my migraines that I released, relating to one pathway of my brain that I rewired.

But I still had more to go.

Chapter 14
Hearing Voices

The point in the beginning of a healing journey, when we first start seeing signs of recovery, is what I call the Pink Light. This is the time in which we feel initial relief from our pain. After long periods of suffering, experiencing symptom relief feels like ecstasy—like freedom and hope. In my experience, this is the time when, if we are destined to become a healer, that we hear the calling to help others through their journeys. I believe that God sets it up this way so that people won't forget to help others. We get this jumpstart of sorts and inspiration to teach what we have learned and to share our stories.

For me, I was already running One Mission, the charity I had founded with Ari, but I was feeling the pull to take helping others to another level. So, in 2014, I started Veda Healing, a Reiki practice on the side.

I started One Mission in 2009, a few years after Nicholas finished treatment. One Mission is a pediatric cancer charity that helps families get through the nightmare of cancer through programs like music therapy, financial assistance, arts and craft therapy, catered meals, and more. Starting a business from the ground up is an exhausting responsibility. I was Human Resources, Tech Support, Sales, *and* Marketing. Eventually, I hired staff, but for the first four years, I ran the charity out of my home with the help of a very good friend, Melissa.

I knew One Mission was one of my life's purposes. I was called to take a horrible situation and turn it into a way to help others. One Mission not only helped me to heal, but it also brought me to other ways I could help families. At first, I offered free Reiki to One Mission families out of my office. I brought in a fuzzy white rug, a massage table, and my crystals, and in between budget meetings, billboard concept meetings, and writing radio scripts, I would turn my office into a healing space. I couldn't think of a better way to help parents who were going through exactly what I went through than to share with them how I healed.

Eventually, my Veda Healing practice grew, and I needed to move out of the One Mission office space. So, I split up my week. I spent two days on Veda Healing and three days on One Mission. I moved the charity into a building where I had a healing office on the floor below the One Mission space. It was so easy to go between office spaces. I loved being able to help the parents of our One Mission families by giving them free Reiki. It made me feel like I was doing exactly what God wanted me to do: help his children. Subconsciously, it was also how I put good karma in the bank. I thought that maybe if I helped people enough, my family would be spared another health crisis.

So, how long does the Pink Light phase last? For some, it can last months or years. As I mentioned above, it often happens in the first stage of healing, which is usually the bumpiest, so oftentimes people get stuck here. My Pink Light phase morphed in the first few years of my healing. I became a healer quickly after I entered into my own healing—something that I don't recommend to others when I offer advice. Healing was a natural talent for me, and I believed it was a sign from God that he was helping me to feel better. So, I took it upon myself to share "the good news" with others, even before I made steady progress on my own path.

What many people don't understand about becoming a healer is that you are *never* not doing your own healing. In my case, I had bucketloads of trauma to unpack, and I had yet to begin. I felt I had completed some of the other heavier items such as losing my mother, and getting through Nicholas's journey, but I had yet to heal my childhood wounds. Still, even when you think you have finished or gotten through a big issue in your life, BAM, it will surface back up again. Healing happens petal by petal—slow and steady, layer by layer. There are many stages to healing the same wound;

and there is no way to change the healing process or trajectory. Instead, healing happens when the time is right.

I am glad that I became a Reiki Master, and I still use Reiki almost every day. At the beginning, it was a little rough for me. A Reiki Master—in my case, Lucinda—is the teacher who passes on the gift of Reiki into and onto the student through a process called Reiki Attunement. As defined by Reiki.com:

> The Reiki attunement is a powerful spiritual experience. The attunement energies are channeled into the student through the Reiki Master. The process is guided by the Rei or God-consciousness and makes adjustments in the process depending on the needs of each student. The attunement is also attended by Reiki guides and other spiritual beings who help implement the process. Many report having mystical experiences involving personal messages, healings, visions, and past life experiences.

Getting my Reiki Attunement opened me up energetically... In fact, too energetically. A few short weeks after my certification, I called Lucinda crying, asking her to shut it down.

"Make it stop," I cried. "This is too much." I begged her to come to my house.

Here's what happened. I'd left a full shopping cart at Stop & Shop because the voices were too much for me. While standing at the deli counter, I heard the woman next to me say something. She was on my left side, which is my deaf side, so I casually said to her, "Sorry, what did you say?" The woman looked at me blankly and told me that she had not said a word. It happened again with the man to my right in the cereal aisle. And I kept hearing people around me talking to me! It soon became clear I was hearing the voices of spirits, not the people around me in aisle five. I panicked. I was so totally freaked out that I left my shopping cart full of groceries and ran right out of the store.

Lucinda laughed after I explained what happened. *She laughed!* I did not find it funny. She explained to me that it was bound to happen to me at some point in my life, because she had known from the first day she put her hands on me at the hair salon that I had "the gift." Being an empath and highly sensitive person (HSP) is a gift. I can see it as such now. But when it first opened up, I would have gladly returned the gift for a life that was not so tuned in, if you catch my drift.

Once I began giving Reiki to clients, I found being highly sensitive and being open to the other side helped me help other people on their own healing journeys. The gift allowed me to be able to channel messages from The Universe that helped my clients gain wisdom during difficult times, connect with loved ones who had passed on, and open their bodies to receive the pure white healing light that The Universe has in abundance for us all.

I know from experience that embarking on a healing journey can be lonely, and being able to help others through my Reiki practice as they, too, felt raw, naked, and alone in the midst of the shifting universe was what I felt called to do. For me, once I got certified to practice Reiki, I was off and running on a new start-up business—and a continued healing path for myself.

However, The Universe was about to shift on me again, and I didn't see it coming.

Learning Reiki was just another distraction for me to not do the deep healing that I truly needed to do. Reiki came naturally to me, and when I found how easy it was for me to help people heal, I focused on them and not on myself. My own healing was on a surface level. I was working full time at One Mission, and now I had a part-time healing practice while doing my usual hand holding of a few cancer parents that came my way.

I am the magnet for all things related to cancer. When people have a friend whose child is diagnosed, they call me. When adults in my life get sick with cancer, they call me. In both cases, I do whatever I can to help. I help the adults get appointments at Dana Farber Cancer Institute; I talk to the parents of sick children and help them emotionally so they can focus on their sick child. I spend countless hours on the phone, pacing around my house or office while I listen to the crying and fear of these people. Of course, I don't simply hang up and go about my day. I hold onto a little piece of each family I help. That is a lot of little pieces of pain and suffering to hold onto while you still haven't done your own healing.

My Reiki clients were an energetic break from my own life—or so I thought.

There are many reasons I am a good helper. One, God made me this way. He gave me a strong body, a loud voice, and a kind heart—all to lead people to get involved, hold people up when they are falling, and to love them all while doing it. Two, I never gave up on helping those in need. Albeit, this was driven by my own dark insecurities, but people were benefitting from my help, nonetheless. I was running toward trying to show people I was good. Good people help, good people listen, good people put themselves aside to help their fellow humans. I wanted to be good. I wanted to be good because I was raised to think I was bad. I wanted to be good because I wasn't loved for being me—being me didn't make her love me.

For a long time, I had no idea that I was killing myself trying to prove I was good. I get it now; I am a good person just as I am in this moment. I don't need to help one more person in order to be good. Today, I help when I am able; when I feel up to it, when I am not already toppled over with helping others. I can help people today while remembering that their crisis is not my emergency.

I loved guiding people through their own healing. Seeing their growth and happiness unfold before me was incredibly rewarding. What happened more often than not was that my clients kept coming back to me, looking for me to heal them. However, they wouldn't do the homework I asked them to do, nor would they be taking the driver's seat in their journey. In other words, I was doing all their work for them.

So, I did it because I could, and they appeared to not be able to. That was a Pink Light misconception on my part. I believed that it was my duty to help them because I had the tools and they had not yet built the abilities. I was dead wrong. It was never my job to do all the work for my clients; it was my job to hold them responsible for their own healing and show them the way. I was so in awe with what I could do in my sessions; so grateful for my own healing ability that I got lost in what the real goal was—to inspire people to take hold of their own journey.

Thankfully, I have more balance now. When I am asked to help, I offer assistance, sharing the tools I used during my own ups and downs with people. And then, I wait for them to call back with questions. When they call back, I know they are ready to take the wheel.

Then I become a passenger—a witness to their story and not the author.

Part 2

Crash and Burn

Chapter 15
The Wheels are Coming Off the Bus

Twelve years after Nicholas was in the hospital, as I was headed into my own healing crisis, which I had no idea was coming. I took on a few of the hardest clients I have ever had, and they sent my nervous system into a frenzy.

Reiki is a hands-on healing modality where, as a healer, I channel the energy from The Universe through my body and out of my hands into the client. This universal energy is pure and very healing. I usually leave out the word God when I'm talking with my clients, but it is the energy of God in my mind.

It wasn't the actual Reiki that was difficult for me with these clients, because letting God's grace flow through me felt natural, and I did this well. It was hearing their stories and holding space for their trauma—that was the most difficult. It caused me to relive my own trauma, though I was unaware of it at the time.

For almost a year, my Veda Healing work looked something like this.

Meet Tyler. Tyler was in his 20s and had some of the worst trauma I had ever heard of. He was molested as a child by his uncle, raped as a teenager, and pretty much got lost in the world of drugs and alcohol from the time he was 15. He found love, got married to another addict, and their baby girl died in her first year of life. When I met Tyler, he was struggling with his sobriety in a big way. He tried to commit suicide at one point and learned to cut himself while in treatment for depression. In spite of all of this, he smiled at me every time he came in for a session. He didn't have a job because he had a hard time holding one down with his depression. He could barely get out of bed each day. My heart ached for him.

The first time I worked on him, I almost threw up in my trash barrel. Feeling someone else's trauma in your body is totally different than feeling your own. When we experience our own trauma, there is a part of us that shuts down, specifically NOT to feel. When you are an energy healer and you are putting your hands on someone, you are purposefully not shut down. In fact, it is the exact opposite: you are wide open.

The thing about healing people is that simply being there for them and holding space for them is healing in and of itself. But for me, I always went deeper with my clients. Why? To be honest, it was because I could. I had the talent and the psychic abilities. It also felt validating to finally be really good at something. I had the emotional intelligence to know what their bodies were telling me, and I used that to help them talk. My psychic abilities came naturally—so naturally that I also knew the stories of people standing next to me at the market or in the line at Starbucks.

Sounds cool, right? Everyone wants to be psychic, until they are.

Tyler didn't sit down the first day and tell me he was raped, or by whom. He didn't even tell me that he cut himself. I had to feel those scars under his long-sleeved shirt. During our second session, I pulled up his sleeve and cried tears on his arm and held my hand on his heart chakra until he also cried. Oftentimes, people simply need permission to cry. It is a delicate balance of push and hold when working with clients who have had extreme trauma. You have to be careful not to rip them open energetically because if they feel too raw, they don't feel safe. When trauma clients don't feel safe, they flee. I learned a dance of balance working with my clients to allow them to open and heal on their own time.

What I was *not* good at was holding space for them while not taking on their pain and holding it in my body like it was mine.

Another one of my challenging clients was a woman slightly older than me who was in what I like to call "The world doesn't make sense to me anymore" crisis. You and I can call her Kim.

I have found over the years working with people that when you come to the point in your life when you don't feel motivated to work, feel lonely in your marriage, or simply want more from life and can't figure out what it means, you are in the process of an energy shift and may have past trauma to work through. It is never too late to heal old trauma. We become ready to heal when the time is right. My oldest client was 75 years old; it's never too late.

In the yogic traditions, old traumas are called samskaras, literally meaning scars or blocks that have formed in your energy body that block the natural flow of energy through and around your body. As souls, we come into human bodies to experience ourselves and we do this through learning and growing as a part of our relationships, family, work, and physical sicknesses. Just like a river, our energy is designed to keep constant flow in our bodies. Rivers flow into lakes and oceans, and then water evaporates into the air. It then rains and fills up the rivers and lakes, and the cycle keeps on moving. When humans create a dam in the river, does the water stop moving? No, it flows up and around into areas where there is no constriction.

Our energy is the same—it will find a place to flow even if it was not originally meant to flow in that area of our bodies. When our energy isn't flowing properly, or into the correct areas of our bodies, it is because we have blocks (samskaras). It is our soul's desire to clear the blocks, and to flow in natural order easily and effortlessly. Our emotions should flow like a free river—*if* we allow them to. There are many reasons we constrict the flow of our energy. As children, we may have been told we are too loud, asked too many questions, or perhaps we were abused in some way, or abandoned. There is usually always a childhood incident, or situation we can tie back to our current thought patterns about how we feel, when we feel, or if we feel our emotions at all.

The first step is to acknowledge that feelings are good. Even feeling emotions that we have labeled bad, such as anger, are good to feel. It means we are alive. It is what we *think* about the emotion that can create a blockage. If we think *I shouldn't feel this way*, or *I don't have the right to feel this way*, or *I am pathetic or weak for feeling this way*, we are stopping the natural flow of emotions. The soul is here to clean up and release the incidents that created the thought about the emotion which is blocking the natural flow state.

In emotionally healthy people, emotions come up and flow away all day, every day. It is when we suppress them that emotions became unhealthy and cause us harm. When we have energetic blockages, our emotions get stuck and they fester, growing like the energy of a fire.

If we are lucky, our emotions pop back up in the form of more emotions, not actions or physical symptoms. In my case, because I wasn't allowed to express my emotions as a child, I grew up repressing them. Then, they came back in the form of chronic pain. They were screaming for my attention for years.

"Listen to me," said the 5-year-old me, "I need to tell you how scared I am feeling." I didn't listen. Again, she came back around when I was 15. "Please let me tell you how angry I am. Will you listen?" she asked me.

Nope. I pushed her right down with some weed and a few beers.

My behavior of repressing emotions was similar to that of my client Kim, who had so much to her story yet barely shared any of it. Nobody ever gave her permission to tell her story or told her that feelings were important. I would often ask her at the beginning of our sessions what she hoped to get out of our session together. She always replied the same way, saying, "I feel so much better after you work on me. I just want to relax."

Working on her was not easy for me because I saw her life in my mind's eye like a movie. I knew that she was raped, I knew that her husband was abusing her, and I knew she was crying all the time when she was alone. I would ask her open-ended questions, like, "How are things going with your husband? How have you been emotionally since our last session?" She always replied to me with a trite "Great, and things are good!"

My job as her healer was to process the energy that was stored in her body, to literally let it flow through me to relieve her. She may never talk about her trauma, or ever admit to anyone that her husband was abusing her. Whether or not she discussed her trauma with me, she was healing, but it was a much slower progression of healing, which some of us need. While it was frustrating for me to not be able to openly discuss what I knew she was going through, it wasn't my place. I had to allow Kim to heal at her own pace and not impose my wishes and desires onto her.

Witnessing another's trauma and allowing them to share their story (when they want to share) is the most precious mutual human experience we can offer to another. It is beyond difficult to do, as most people go into relate mode, sharing their story too. What is most profound is to listen, to really listen.

I was listening to all of my clients tell me their stories and absorbing them. I took their stories home and thought about them in between sessions. I lacked emotional boundaries and self-care, which is why I was headed into my own healing crisis.

Re-traumatization is when your body is triggered by a current situation, which results in a re-experiencing of the initial trauma event. It can be triggered by a situation, an attitude or expression, or by certain environments that replicate the dynamics of the original trauma, like loss of power or control, or feeling unsafe.

From the moment I founded One Mission and walked back into the hospital where we lived with Nicholas, either for One Mission meetings or to meet families who requested my help, I was re-traumatizing my nervous system with each trip. I knew I was anxious walking the halls of the hospital, I knew that it was affecting me, but I didn't understand how or what the mechanics were. I had no idea the level of abuse I was doing to my nervous system. No idea.

When I would visit families in the hospital, even the alarm sounds of the IV pumps would make me twitch. The smells, the sounds, the feelings and emotions were all sending my body back into fight or flight. At the time, I simply shrugged off my anxiety in these situations. I assumed I was just uncomfortable being back in the hospital again, and when I would leave, I would feel better, so I just kept going. I didn't even give it a second thought.

I have been to seven child funerals, including my own niece. Death, suffering, loss, and sadness was the world I lived in. For 10 years, I was consistently re-triggering my old traumas. Since my body endured years and years of trauma, it makes sense then that it would take me years to recover.

I usually take the fast track in life—I buy the VIP tickets, I pay for the curbside pick-up and drop off; in and out as fast as possible. I have people to see and places to go. But when it came to healing my own trauma, there was no fast lane I could pull into, no VIP ticket experience, and no easy in and easy out. The fast lane didn't exist.

Are you attempting to speed your way through your healing and recovery like I was?

Perhaps you've even been feeling emotions and physical symptoms pop up as you've read my stories thus far and pushed them down.

First off, you're not alone. Second, I want you to remember that there is no timeline on healing. It will happen as slow or as fast as it needs to, and you cannot rush it. However slow it takes, you can, and you will heal.

Chapter 16
The Beginning of the End

*D*uring the time when my clients were coming in with very intense and difficult issues to work on, I began not feeling well again. One early fall evening in 2018, as I drove home from One Mission, I began getting a severe headache. By the time I pulled into the driveway, I couldn't see. My vision seemed as if I had smeared Vaseline all over my eyeballs, and I could barely make out my own hands. I staggered up the walkway and grasped at walls as I crawled inside and went straight to bed. These headaches were happening almost weekly, and the episodes of vertigo that came with them would last for a few days. I was either in migraine hell or vertigo limbo. I never felt good, and my panic was starting to rebuild. All my old fears were coming back. Something was terribly wrong with me; my body was defying me.

I tried to tell my husband something was wrong with me, but he brushed it off. For years after we got married, I went from doctor to doctor, always complaining of something weird and unique. I must have sounded like a broken record to him. Ari and I are different people with different approaches to fear and anxiety. I needed to talk through my fears, while Ari rarely admitted he had any. So, I had no real outlet. I was lonely, and at times, I would suffer in silence. In many ways, it was easier for me to be alone with my pain instead of showing my vulnerability to my husband, leaving him unsure of a good response, which is why he brushed off my conviction that something was wrong with me.

On top of that, Ari was in the middle of a crisis at work, one that we couldn't tell anyone about. His family had decided that they wanted to sell Cumberland Farms, their 80-year-old family business, and it was his job to handle the sale. He couldn't tell any of his employees, and had to run the business day to day as if everything were normal. He was struggling, and his stress level was off the charts.

We were both in crisis at the same time. Our marriage had weathered the storm of a crisis before when Nicholas was ill, but this was different. When Nicholas was ill, it presented as something for Ari and I to focus on as a team. When I became sick years later, we had a difficult time being on the same team, and there was nothing else to focus on except for the large void that was growing between us.

I was desperate for answers and began getting test after test. I had X-rays of my sinus cavity, thinking that I had chronic sinusitis, and perhaps that was causing my headaches. I had MRIs of my back and neck, hoping to find a reason for my incapacitating dizzy spells. All the tests were coming back negative, and even the MRI of my brain was normal. I was dumbstruck. How could I be experiencing this level of pain this regularly and not have an anatomical or physical problem that could lead to a diagnosis? Why was my body doing this, and how could not one of the doctors figure it out?

Each time I sat on the cold table at the doctor's office in my paper gown, I would start with, "I don't know, this could be anxiety, but…" I think a part of me knew I was coming undone due to stress. The other part of me couldn't understand that, because I thrived in stressful situations. I was the FIXER, for God's sake. I was the person everyone came to with their problems, and I healed people with my own hands. I built a company, raised three children, took care of two homes, was a support system to my husband like every other good wife of a CEO, and on and on. I wasn't supposed to be the broken one. I couldn't put the puzzle pieces together. What changed? Why was stress now affecting me this negatively?

By the end of 2018, I had to start canceling my client sessions, and soon, I was canceling everything. My headaches were daily, and my vertigo left me bedridden.

An episode I had at the end of January 2019 changed everything: my marriage, my relationships with my friends, and my ability to run One

Mission—so much so that I tried to quit. The episode's effects were massive, and to this day, thinking about it makes me dizzy with anxiety.

I'd gone to bed the night before with a bad migraine and I was exceptionally dizzy. Like, drunken bed spin dizzy. Ari's movement as he got into bed made my vertigo much worse. I couldn't take it. I asked him to sleep in the guest bedroom. I would have gone myself, but I didn't think I could get up. He huffed out of the room, and I lay there worried he was mad at me. I don't think he understood how awful I felt, but his frustration was palpable, and I felt I had done something wrong by asking him to leave. He was leaving the next morning on a flight to go fishing in Venezuela. The trip was part work, part fun.

It was 3 a.m. I remember that because Ari had come in to get dressed to leave for his flight. Something was very wrong with me—I couldn't tell where I was in the bed. I was disoriented. I opened my eyes and everything in my vision had shifted to the right. What normally was on the ceiling was on the right wall, and what was normally on the right wall was down by the bed on the floor. Nothing made sense. I screamed for Ari to help me.

"Help me get back on the bed. Oh my God, where am I? What is wrong with me?"

The most difficult thing about vertigo and migraines is that they are invisible. Ari had no idea what I was talking about. To him I was on the bed and my head was on the pillow. Following my orders, he tried to pick me up and position me on the pillow, but it felt like I was free-falling down 50 stories. I was grabbing his arms so tightly that I scratched him with my nails, and he yelled at me to stop. He got me back in bed and finished getting his stuff together for his trip.

He is going to leave me like this, I thought, and immediately began crying. I had never been so scared before. He called our nanny and asked her to come over, and then he left. He said goodbye, that he would check on me before he boarded the flight, and then I heard the front door close.

That is when I began to vomit.

"He left me, he left me, he left me."

Chapter 17
Alone

I could not love any man more than I love my husband. Our love was straight out of a Danielle Steel novel, full of passion, depth and connection. I believe that we were destined to be together for so many reasons, our son Nicholas being one of them. We were a power couple. We lifted one another up and rooted for the home team, and we had a bond that many people envied. Nothing mattered more to us than each other. We were perfectly happy to stay home, enjoy a bottle of wine, and talk for hours rather than go out with friends. Meeting Ari in 1998 was the best thing that ever happened to me.

Early on in our relationship, he taught me to see in myself the person everyone else saw: a beautiful and amazing woman. My husband brought out my best qualities—my strength, power, and drive to succeed. He is also the only man on earth that can take me to my knees with one wrong word, or by leaving me alone when I was at my sickest.

Our love helped me to soar high. More often than not, I felt he loved me unconditionally, and he often told me how much he loved me.

But he abandoned me when I needed him the most, and I was shattered.

As I continued to be sick for hours, and the room continued to move and shift on me, I couldn't for the life of me figure out why he didn't love me enough to stay. *I must not be a good enough wife*, I thought to myself.

I would never do this to him. I would never leave. If he truly loved me, he would have stayed. It was simple for me; if you love someone, you put yourself aside to care for them. So, I was confused: how could I be so grounded in our love, so certain of it being sacred and real, and yet at the same time feel so abandoned? I hated that I was questioning our love, but nothing else made sense to me. What was going through his head? The woman he loves so dearly was sick and frail, and somehow in his mind, it was OK to leave.

Years later, after many months in therapy, I learned it was black and white thinking that had me questioning our love. It was black and white thinking that led me to think that because he left, he didn't love me.

That is precisely how my thinking has always been. I either like you or I don't. I am either in or out. I am either dieting or binging. And I don't fake anything. Ever. The problem with my thinking in this way is that life isn't black or white. It has 50 shades of gray!

My black and white thinking began in childhood. It happened naturally around the age of 10, when my mother and I began not getting along. It is normal for children to think this way because their brains are still developing, and life experience is minimal. It is also a survival mechanism built into our brains—it is primitive.

When children get hungry, they ask for food. When children are sad, they cry. When a parent smiles and loves a child, that child feels safe. Simple, primitive thinking.

My black and white thinking, on the other hand, was born out of neglect and fear. It was simple for me: my mother didn't love me because she would leave me home alone and she would yell at me. When she would drink, she would get mean, and I wasn't safe from her painful words or sullen neglect. This thought process became habitual for me, and when I got older, I used this method to survive. My brain learned to use this thinking as a way to keep me safe in all situations. When my mother was in a bad mood, I knew that she would come after me, so I would make myself invisible by hiding in my room. When she was in a bad mood, it meant she would hurt me.

I used this simplistic way of thinking to keep myself out of harm's way. When adults with childhood trauma grow older, we present as hypervigilant, always seeing the negative side of things. On occasion, we are referred to as

"Debbie Downers." This isn't because we are depressed or don't like people. It is because our brains were simply wired for survival; analyzing people and places for safety. For some, big crowds mean danger, backaches mean a tumor, and words like "always" and "never" are used to describe fleeting emotions or situations.

The day of my big episode with the dizzying migraine, in my mind, it was absolutely clear to me—my husband didn't love me because if he did, he wouldn't have left me. That was black and white thinking, and not for one second did it reflect Ari's feelings or words. I assumed that he couldn't have loved me when he chose to get on his flight. What I forgot to consider was that he had zero tools to know how to take care of me. We need to be shown as children how to have empathy for others, and Ari was not raised to have empathy for anyone—he was raised to compete and survive.

I never took into consideration that he was terrified and frozen with how sick I was, nor thought that he had never been sick like that himself. I felt like he was allergic to me; my being sick repelled him somehow. He had no idea what I was feeling, and no one had ever taken care of him in the way I needed him to take care of me, so how could he possibly know how to do it himself?!

He did love me and felt guilty and conflicted about going on the trip, but I didn't know that. My brain didn't know that either.

Black and white thinking robs you of the ability to consider other options. It robs you of the facts. It took me a long time to unravel my black and white thinking, and it still pops back up from time to time. Letting go of it happened naturally when I began healing my inner child. Once I began making connections to trapped emotions and their original trauma, I was able to see how my brain was stuck in the past. It was through this work that I was able to see how my brain was still in survival mode.

Our love was and continues to be very strong. While we worked out the trauma of this time in our marriage, over dinner one night I cried, telling him how I feared that he didn't love me when he left that night. I explained how I worry that when he is angry, it is because of me.

"Ashley, I always love you. My life is you, I always love you," he said calmly.

I asked him to repeat himself, and then I really started to cry. "I always love you," he said. "Even when I am mad, even when I make mistakes like not taking care of you when you need me to. I always love you."

"Write that down on a napkin right now!" I said through my tears. I had an idea.

He did, and then a week later, I had his words tattooed, in his handwriting, on my right arm so that I could always see it.

Observation is a gift from God, it changes everything. Ari and I continue to learn together how and why we both have black and white thinking. We are dedicated to our marriage, and we both openly discuss our triggers through the gift of observation.

The simple task of observing my triggers allows me the space to see the present moment for what it is. Ari leaving me that night reminded my brain of my mother, so it went into defense mode, turning on the black and white thinking. Childhood neglect is a long road of healing. Just when you think you have healed a wound, it will likely pop back up again later in a different form. It did for me.

Chapter 18
Answers

The next day, I got a call from my friend Taylor. He had heard about my migraines from our mutual friend Robin, and I was moved that he took the time to reach out to me—he was doing so from the ESPN set in between live segments. Taylor is an MLS soccer commentator, and a mighty funny one at that.

Taylor began asking me all sorts of questions. "Where is the pain? Can you watch TV? Can you use your phone? Do lights bother you? What color lights? How is your anxiety level? When you close your eyes, what do you feel in your eye sockets?"

So many questions…

I answered them in rapid fire. "No, I cannot use my phone, it makes my brain hurt. I am wearing sunglasses around the house because the sunlight pouring into my windows hurts, too. My anxiety is off the charts. Taylor, what if I never get better? What is even wrong with me? When I close my eyes, my eyeballs are dancing around in my sockets, they never rest."

"Your brain is broken," he said. "You need my guy Pedro to fix it. Trust me. He is the best, and I know because I have been at this for 10 years."

Taylor played professional soccer for years, but his career ended with a devastating concussion—the last one of many. After his soccer career ended, he endured years of migraines and vertigo. He knew what I was feeling, and that made me trust him. He referred me to his chiropractor neurologist, Dr. Victor Pedro. I got an appointment for the following week.

Dr. Pedro (I eventually nicknamed him Pedro as Taylor did) was a brilliant Portuguese man who appeared both intense and nurturing at the same time. My first appointment was three hours in which Pedro performed three different tests on me. The first was a balance platform test, where I closed my eyes and turned my head in five different directions. The platform I was standing on was designed to pick up the movements in my feet, recording my shifts in balance. I failed three of the five balance tests. I completely fell off the platform! Normal brain scores are in the 80s to 90s, and my brain was scoring in the low 60s. No wonder I felt dizzy!

The second test was the Interactive Metronome. They carefully placed big headphones over my ears, and I listened to a cowbell accompaniment while trying to time the beat with a clicker in my hand. I was clacking like a maniac, trying to keep the beat. I failed that test miserably, too, with the lowest score you could get.

The final test was a set of video goggles that filmed my eye movements while I stared at buzzing lines on the wall. I could feel my eyes bugging out of my head. My brain was frantic, and my eyes told the story.

Going over the scores with Pedro was a low point for me. He sat me down, looked me in the eye, and said, "Your anxiety is off the charts, and it's making you sick. You have migraines, yes, and I know the part of your brain that is weak. That I can fix. But if you don't get your anxiety under control, you will never feel better." He went on to explain that anxiety lives in the same part of your brain that migraines originate from before dropping another bombshell.

"Your symptoms are more than 50 percent anxiety."

I was shocked. *Shocked.* No way was my anxiety that bad! "So, what you're telling me is that I made myself sick?"

"Well, you didn't make yourself sick, your anxiety did."

I saw Pedro the very next day for treatment and remained in his care for three months. Without him, I would not have my life back today. In the beginning, treatment was miserable. I had to travel from Massachusetts to Rhode Island three times a week, and my symptoms got worse with all the driving. I was having a hard time trusting that Pedro was going to help me, but with each session, my trust with him was building. I didn't generally trust people, so this was a big step.

After my second week in treatment, Pedro told me that traveling was holding me back from getting better because by the time I arrived after the hour drive to his office, my brain was already tired from all of the stimulation of the cars passing by, the sun shining in my eyes, and of course, the anxiety about all of it. Most of his patients move from all over the country to Rhode Island for the length of their treatment, staying at a local hotel close by, making for an easy drive to treatment daily.

Pedro said move, so I did.

With the specialized treatment which he called Cortical Integrative Therapy (CIT), he was able to pinpoint the area of my brain that was injured. We think the straw that broke the camel's back was from an old concussion that I reinjured the spring before my migraines started. When I was in high school, I was in a car accident, and during the collision, I hit my head on the rearview mirror and knocked the mirror completely off. That was my first concussion. My second one came from a head blow to the side of my car as I was entering after a very turbulent plane flight. It was an extremely windy day and my balance was off from the flight. The combination of the wind blowing the car door as I attempted to slide into the car, and my leaning forcefully with all of my body's weight to sit inside, was the perfect recipe for a head injury. I tried to get in the car fast and misjudged the clearance for my head. BAM.

I had a headache for weeks after that blow.

Science tells us that the more concussions you have, the easier it is to get them, meaning the less force or impact is needed to jar your brain in subsequent head injuries. It may have been hitting my head that kicked off the migraines, but the underlying issue of anxiety and stress were just waiting to cause me problems. Because the part of our brain which experiences migraines is the same part of the brain where anxiety lives, that cycle just keeps going and going for a chronic migraine sufferer. Anxiety, migraine. Migraine, anxiety.

Treatment consisted of wearing a STIM muscle stimulator unit; a type of a TENS unit (Transcutaneous Electrical Nerve Stimulation). To use a TENS unit you place the small sticky pads anywhere on your body, and they send mild electrical current into your muscles. Pedro first placed the STIM unit on me during my initial platform test after I had fallen off. He stopped the test and placed the pads on my wrists and face. I got back on the platform and my score was almost perfect. By re-testing me while wearing the unit, Pedro knew which part of my brain was injured.

Some physical therapists use TENS units to bring blood flow to areas of the body that are recovering from injury. For my treatments with Pedro, I would place the sticky pads on various spots on my body: one on my jaw line, one on the top of my shoulder, and one on the inside and outside of my wrists. For my legs, I placed two pads on the outside edges of my ankles and same for my knees. Then I would wrap warm wet towels over my arm and leg, which were designed to calm my nervous system down; to dampen (no pun intended) the overexcited part of my brain that was causing me symptoms.

We treated my left side because it was the right side of my brain that was weak. Though it might sound counterintuitive, the right side of our brain controls the left side of our bodies. As you might conclude, Pedro diagnosed that the right side of my brain was the side where I had the injury.

As I progressed, I would wear the TENS unit and stare at a wall that had moving lines on it, and then I used the interactive metronome that synced my body to my brain. The action of clicking the button on the beat of the cow bell syncs both sides of your brain, and by doing this with your hands, it helps your physical body talk to your brain so they are speaking the same language. At first, the metronome would exhaust me. I could barely get through each session without having to take breaks and sit down. When my brain would get tired from trying to stay on beat, my physical body would get symptoms of headache and dizziness.

Towards the end of my treatment, I could fly through the metronome sessions with ease and swiftness. Even random everyday things were therapy for me, like riding on an escalator. Pedro had me ride the escalator in my hotel daily while wearing my TENS unit, and I dreaded it. I was exhausted after my double sessions with him, and people would stare at me. I had the TENS pads on my face and wrists, wires every which way. Oh, you know, just hanging out riding the escalator over and over again. I looked like a mental patient! I actually felt like one at the time, too. My outer appearance and inner monologue were matching perfectly.

I had an hour session in the morning and an hour session in the afternoon. Pedro monitored my heart rate and oxygen levels during treatment to determine if I was taxing my brain too much. I remember asking him every session, "When will I get better? When will this go away?"

He would always reply, "Ashley, you are better. You are getting better."

It was hard for me to understand because I still felt so awful, that I was not able to see how far I had come. My fear and anxiety were preventing me from living in the moment and celebrating small things, like being able to sit up for two hours on the couch after treatment before I had to go lie down again.

In the early days of treatment, I would throw up in buckets and barely make it through my sessions without crying. It sounds pathetic, but I felt so awful when I first started that I would need to go lay down in a dark room afterward and not come out until the next day. As weeks went by, I started smiling during treatments and would joke around with the staff. A far cry from where I started! Early on, I was all business: get in, get out. Everyone around me could see I was getting better.

But I couldn't see it because I didn't *feel* it. I wasn't living in the present moment. Instead, I was stuck in repetitive thought: I am sick, I am sick. I wanted to feel like I did before I got sick, before migraines entered my life and before I was throwing up in buckets with a guy named Pedro. I wanted to be better so badly, but all I thought about was the fact that I *was* sick. Many of us do this—try to get back to where we were before the crisis. However, that is not why we endure the crisis in the first place. To get back to where we were would mean that we stayed put and didn't move forward. In this case, I was holding onto a part of me that no longer existed. She had changed.

On top of everything, the pressure I felt to be a good wife was beginning to weigh heavily on me. My husband was in a nightmare situation at work and I wasn't capable of being there for him emotionally, nor was I even physically living in Massachusetts. We were so far apart, both geographically and energetically. We would talk briefly while I was in treatment in Rhode Island, but it was chit-chat. *How are you, how are the kids?* I was feeling alone and scared, and I felt like I was failing my husband. I missed him. I missed our marriage, our closeness, his touch.

Pedro released me in April when my platform scores were in the mid 80s (compared to my initial scores of low 60s) and I was balanced. He was pleased with how my treatment progressed, and there was a small part of me that was, too. But as I drove home from my last session with him, I felt like a scared schoolgirl waiting in the hallway for her bully to pass by. I was waiting for the next shoe to drop.

I had no idea how to trust that I was going to be OK, because the unknown was always an unsafe place for me growing up. I was programmed to prepare for the future by seeing it as bleak or bad so that I wouldn't be disappointed. Children need two things while growing up in order to feel safe.

1. Unconditional Love.
2. Attachment.

By the time I hit junior high, I was pretty clear that my mother really never wanted to have me, and if we were attached at all, it was bonded in toxicity. Life in general became scary to me, including but not limited to school sleepovers, my mother, and her unpredictable behavior. In the case of my migraines, not knowing what was coming next was super scary, so I rehearsed my tragedy. All I thought about was the big vertigo episode, and I constantly worried that it would happen again. I was rehearsing in my mind that I was sick, that the vertigo was going to come back, and my life was never going to get back on track. I lived in fear, and I was afraid to do anything. This vicious cycle continued for almost a year. My brain thought it was protecting me by thinking about the big episode it was preparing me to deal with when it happened. There were days it almost did happen.

When I got home from treatment with Pedro, life was different, and I felt lost. This was the part of my journey I call the blank slate. I wiped everything off my plate. Everything. I wasn't working at One Mission everyday as I had before I got sick, and I stopped taking clients at Veda Healing. I barely saw or talked to my friends, and my husband and I were living like roommates. I was alone and stripped of everything I knew to be "me." It was my rock bottom.

The good news was there was only one way out, and that was up.

I was scared; lost without a map. I would walk around the house while the kids were in school like a confused Alzheimer's patient. I had nowhere to go, no calls to make, no meetings to attend—I didn't even know who I was anymore. This was beyond anxiety provoking, which was a problem because I now knew that my anxiety was making me sick. It was a vicious cycle of feeling lost without any focus except my intrusive negative thoughts, which

I then beat myself up for having. Not to mention I no longer had work to use as an escape. Either way, I was not helping myself get better. So, I sat down and began researching.

I typed "how to treat anxiety naturally" into Google. I got a load of supplement ads, and therapist names at first, but then I stumbled upon some information about the brain activity of PTSD patients. Sticking with the brain made sense to me since I had just left Pedro. I knew I needed to figure out why my brain was stuck on repeat worrying about the past, and I was desperate to figure out how to stay in the present moment.

That was April of 2019, and it took me until October to fully understand how and why my brain and body were so intensely anxious. I wound up studying with Dr. Joe Dispenza, reading his books and taking his online class. It was official, my brain was hard-wired for anxiety through the circumstances of my life. The good news was that Dr. Joe had figured out a way to retrain the brain through deep meditation, so I started there.

Chapter 19
Am I Safe?

Dr. Joe's meditations were deep and impactful, but they were not getting me to where I wanted to be—which was anxiety-free. I was enjoying the meditations but was not reaping the benefits as I think others were, and it was slowly becoming clear to me why.

In order to achieve inner peace, we must clean out the closet. Our bodies are the closet, and unprocessed trauma and repressed emotions are the junk. My closet was overflowing. I simply could not envision a new, healthy, happier me as Dr. Joe had instructed without cleaning out my closet first. I needed a douching of emotions, and to clear out some trauma to make room for a new vision.

A trauma response is the body's way of trying to regulate and to calm down the firing and wiring of the nervous system in its heightened state of arousal. It is trying to gain footing on safe ground. This response can show up in the form of an emotional shutdown, an outburst of anger, an emotional meltdown of tears, rapid heart rate, addiction, or any other behavior that one uses to "feel better." These sensations of hyper arousal in the trauma child were often felt during times of abuse, neglect, and other stressful times. When the adult body feels these sensations, it will do just about anything to escape and flee the situation that is causing them. The difficult concept to understand for the trauma child is distinguishing a present-day moment from a trigger from the past.

Children who are raised by neglectful, abusive, and toxic parents often-times feel unlovable, and thus grow up with a very shaky foundation of self-love, self-care, and emotional regulation. As a consequence, when the spouse of a trauma adult seems distance, distracted, or doesn't show the attention needed, trauma adults often become clingy, distrustful, and will have outbursts and arguments; all in the effort of trying to connect. The connection made by arguments and negative interactions oddly enough feels safe to the adult; because as a child that is the only attention they received from their abusive parent. They also have a skewed view of the world, which can leave them behaving in certain ways incongruent with how they feel. Usually, this is displayed in people pleasing. This was me.

The child who is neglected and abused grows into the adult who can't trust, feels anxious when they slow down, looks for what can go wrong in all situations, and cannot regulate their emotions without the help of alcohol or drugs. This was also me.

It is important to define what the roles of parents are, and what happens in the brain of a child when a parent is not unconditionally loving—or even is not keeping themselves safe, for instance by using drugs and alcohol, or is filled with rage and takes it out on the child. Aside from food, clothing, shelter, and other basic needs, a parent has a big job to fill. Things that are crucial to how a child feels about themselves are: praise, encouragement, understanding the importance of rules, honesty, and the concepts of caring, community, and sharing.

There are loving parents out there who don't encourage their child, per se, and there are parents out there who love their child but don't take them through the lessons of life. We would not define these parents as abusive. We do define it as abuse when a child is neglected, or told they are bad, beaten, sexually abused, or made to fear their parents. In these cases, children have a brain that has stopped developing and gone into survival mode. The brain of an abused child literally stops developing.

When the child, now an adult, is triggered, they will revert into survival mode even if they are truly safe in the moment. For me, it didn't matter that I was no longer living with my abuser. Each and every time I encountered a situation in which I felt abandoned, left out, not good enough, or worse yet, vulnerable, I would go into shutdown mode.

And I mean SHUTDOWN mode.

It used to snow more in the early winter when I was in high school than it does now. Maybe this global warming thing is real.

On this January day, it was lightly snowing, and we were playing our rivals, Natick High, on their court. I played basketball in the winter to keep in shape for volleyball. My volleyball coach was also my basketball coach, and she asked me to join the team. I had zero clue how to play the game; I was clueless. I would run the wrong way down the court trying to make a shot. What made me the slightest bit good at basketball was that I was angry, and I used that anger to push girls aside during rebound shots.

A player from the Natick team had been toying with me all night. She would push me during rebounds, and as she ran by me down the court, she was fucking with me, and I was getting *mad*.

We had only a few minutes left of the third quarter, and I was determined to successfully land the next rebound. We both jumped up, almost shoulder to shoulder. I stretched my hand as far into the sky as I could, and my fingertips brushed the ball—I barely had it in my hand. In that very moment, she pushed me. Again. This time, we were in mid-air.

I could tell that I was over the line, so I turned my body just so slightly so that I could toss the ball to a teammate, trying to keep the play alive. This turn of my body and her push made me land on just one leg, and that force blew my kneecap out of place. I landed on the ground in excruciating pain. I quickly looked down and saw the misalignment, and thus immediately passed out.

As I came to, my coach was standing over me, her voice sounding like Charlie Brown's mother.

Waaah Wahh Wah…

The Natick trainer told me to call my mother. "You definitely blew out your ACL, I watched you land. You need to go to the hospital," she said. I was scared and in excruciating pain. She wrapped me in ice, gave me a pair of crutches, and I hobbled over to the payphone inside the girls' locker room.

"Hey Mom, I need to go to the hospital," I began to cry. "The trainer thinks I blew out my ACL, it really hurts. Can you come and get me?"

"Now?" my mother said. "It's snowing, just take the bus back later and I will get you at school."

The hospital was closer to Natick High than it was to my school; she just didn't want to come and get me. After I hung up, I sat down on the bench and cried.

"Is she coming to get you?" the trainer asked.

"No, she can't right now," I mumbled as I hobbled away on crutches, full of shame.

My mother did pick me up at school later on that night, but she didn't take me to the hospital until the next day. I was in so much pain that I stayed on the couch—I couldn't even make it to my room. I lay up all night getting my own ice packs, watching TV and trying to pass the time. My knee was swollen and getting worse by the hour. My anxiety was sky high, and I was alone. When I called my father, crying in pain, he didn't take me to the hospital either. There was nobody there to care for me; nobody there to protect me. I was alone.

I didn't consciously choose to stop needing my mother in this moment, but I *did* begin to form walls of protection against her not showing up to care for me. In truth, these walls of protection are not real walls. At the core, they are repressed feelings of hurt, anger, loss, and fear. For me, the walls are against my feelings; they are in place to help me to not feel. My emotions were too overwhelming for me to handle, so I just ignored them. Pushed them down as far as I could. This act of repression is commonly known as walls of protection.

What is often misconstrued is that these walls are not formed to protect from actions *against* the child, rather to protect children from how they *feel* about it. Seeing as no one cared for me when I had a physical issue such as needing knee surgery, which I did receive later in that week, there was no way that I could allow myself to feel sad, hurt, or neglected. Children don't have tools to handle emotions this large and this intense; they need the help of a loving adult with them in times of deep sadness, coaching them how to regulate their feelings and calm their bodies. I knew there was no chance I would get that, so in protection, I couldn't allow myself to experience the feelings in the first place.

While this was a decent strategy for survival as a child, it is a horrible coping mechanism as an adult. Adults know how to regulate—they know how to ask for help and then can implement tools for healing. The traumatized child within me needed to be introduced to the capable adult she indeed became.

The following is an excerpt from Khiron Clinics, which is an innovative treatment program of nervous-system informed therapies for patients with PTSD and other anxiety disorders. The clinic is advised by Bessel van de Kolk, Stephen Porges, Deb Dana, Janina Fisher, and Licia Sky. They are located in the UK.

> Coming to the realization that what you viewed as normal was actually very unhealthy is the first step to getting help and support and finding liberation toward a new and healthier way of being. It is crucial for a child's self-worth and self-esteem to have their deepest emotional needs met and to be able to relate to parents on an emotional level. When they are instead met with detachment and constant criticism, it creates an atmosphere of stress and anticipation of punishment, which can have long-term effects on both physical and mental health due to the relentless environment of stress it creates. The good news is that with the appropriate care and support, you can move past this. You can put down that baggage and change the course of history, or even her story.[1]

Learning about PTSD and becoming educated on how my mother treated me (and that it was indeed abusive) has allowed me to heal. Being brought to the hospital after an injury is perhaps one of the most basic needs of a child, and to be left alone in pain to fend for myself was abusive.

After years of this work, I can see as an adult how moments when I experience feelings of neglect, not being good enough to love, or when I become ill, trigger my brain. It goes into shutdown mode in order to protect me from my own feelings about the original situation that caused me to feel these old, trauma-based emotions. Perhaps you can see yourself in this cycle as well.

The work, then, is to bridge the gap between childhood trauma and present-day safety.

---

[1] https://khironclinics.com/

Part 3

Putting the Pieces Together

Chapter 20
Envy

*S*ummertime has always been a special time of year for me and Ari. From the time I started One Mission in 2009 and Ari took over Cumberland Farms in 2010, summer was our favorite season to spend together. We both worked until 6 or 6:30 most nights, rushed home, ate dinner, put the kids to bed and then finished any unfinished work for a few hours before going to bed.

Our usual week looked something like this: business dinners (such as gatherings with the governer), meet and greets with employees or prospective donors, and one of us seemed to always be winning an award of some sort, which meant *another* dinner and speech. This went on for 10 years, never really taking much of a break or vacation. We often spent hours at night in the dead of winter talking about how awesome the upcoming summer was going to be and how we could slow down and enjoy life. Looking back now, I find this remarkable that we were in the prime of our careers, thriving by most cultural standards, and all we talked about was slowing down.

The year 2014 was a great year for both of us. One Mission was thriving, our biggest fundraiser, The Buzz Off for Kids with Cancer, hit $1.1 million in revenue, and Cumberland Farms was growing by multiples never before seen in the history of the company. We went to Cape Cod that June, as we had every summer since 2009, for our traditional summer on the ocean. We'd been there less than four days when I got the call from one of my mother's friends. Joan had been my mother's boss, and they remained close after my mother moved to Florida with her boyfriend during my freshmen year of college.

My mother had a stroke, and Joan thought I should know. "Joan, I have not talked to my mother in almost 11 years," I said. "She and I stopped talking years ago. Last I knew she was still in Florida."

"Your mother has been living in Massachusetts for almost seven years, Ashley," Joan said flatly.

"Wait, what? You are telling me my mother has been living in the same state in which I live, the same state where I have been promoting One Mission, which she has clearly seen on TV or billboards, and she has never reached out to me, not even once?!" I barked at Joan. "What are you asking me to do, go and see her?"

"Ashley, your mother loves you. I just wanted you to know." I hung up and sat on my hardwood kitchen floor, staring at the grains in the wood. My first thought was, *There goes my summer.*

I had not talked to my mother since Nicholas was in the hospital. She had no idea that I had given birth to two amazing little girls—that I had a whole life without her in it. I mourned my mother as if she was dead. So many emotions funneled in at once from the moment Joan and I hung up: fear, worry, unease, and anger. The prospect of having my mother back in my life, and now her not being well was overwhelming to say the least. It was extremely difficult for me to even consider getting in my car and driving to her. I mean, she left me, and I moved on… and now she was back? I didn't want to uproot my life to go see her. It was against my better judgement, and I needed to protect myself.

It was hours later that my guilt kicked into high gear. I don't have any siblings, so if I didn't go to see my mother, who would? I didn't know if my uncles knew what had happened, and the thought of her sick and alone was what got me into my car to drive to see her in some Beverly hospital. I had not seen her face, smelled her perfume, or touched her skin since the day I got married.

With every mile I drove, my body began to tense and tighten. I was feeling sick, and my anxiety was dizzying. The irony was that the route I took to the hospital was lined with digital billboards, and every one of them displayed One Mission advertising for The Buzz Off event we had just hosted the week prior. Our artwork was still in rotation, which was unusual. After the event, the ad usually comes right down.

God was sending me a message billboard after billboard: you are a good person, you are safe, you have a whole life without her in it, and you are OK. Seeing my ads brought me back to reality. They reminded me that I am a grown woman, successful and strong. I sat up straighter, took in a deep breath, and pulled into the hospital parking lot. "I can do this," I told myself. "I can do this." I closed my eyes, trying to calm myself down. However, rather than feeling calm, I was flooded with memories.

I remembered one of the last times I saw my mother. One night during that last Florida trip, we were supposed to have dinner with my mother's boyfriend's brother and his wife. I knew she wanted me to meet their son, and I didn't want to go. "He is cute," she said. "Come with us, I told them you wanted to meet him."

I ended up having the worst panic attack I had ever had. I was dizzy, my heart was racing, and I felt like I was going to be sick. There was a huge knot in my stomach. My palms were sweating, and my legs were shaking. I knew that this boy had a history of drug abuse, and that he was in and out of jail. This was the boy my mother would rather I be with instead of my kind, wholesome, and loving soon-to-be fiancé, Ari.

She sat down next to me on the couch as my body trembled. "You don't have to stay with him if you don't want to, Ashley." She was referring to Ari. Although I was frozen with fear, I realized the woman sitting next to me knew nothing about me. She had no idea that I finally felt alive, loved and cared for. She didn't know that I was living my Danielle Steel novel. But she knew I had something real and good. Everyone knew.

She just didn't want me to have a better life than she had. This realization was crippling me in fear. My mother, the woman who is supposed to love, advocate, and care for me, not only didn't even know me, she would rather I live a miserable life like hers than be happy.

Hospitals. They make me anxious. The smells, the shiny floors, the hustle and bustle, the alarms and overhead announcements. I walked into the hospital and my pace got swifter. I was on my way to the unknown. Would she know who I was when I walked in? Would we talk about the fact we had not talked in years? What would my mother say to me? I was anticipating the moment with so much worry and fear. My palms were sweating, and my stomach was aching.

I opened the door and found her staring at the wall.

"Mom?" I bent my head so she could see my face.

"Bashey," she called to me; the nickname she gave me when I was little. Her ability to speak was not impaired, but her thoughts were a little muddled. She smiled. "You came to see me. I need you to help me. Hand me my pocketbook. I need a cigarette."

"Mom, you can't have a cigarette, you just had a stroke." That made her angry, but I didn't take it personally. I think her stroke was making her antsy. "What happened, Mom? Tell me how you got here."

She went on to explain the events of her previous few weeks, leading up to a visit at a CVS Minute Clinic because she knew she was having a stroke. We talked for an hour, and it was becoming clear to me that she was not going to bring up anything related to us. I was bursting, and I had to ask.

"Mom, it has been a while since we talked."

"That was your choice," she snapped. "Grab me my cellphone, I have to call my boss and tell her that I am not coming to work tomorrow."

"My choice?" I questioned her. Just as I was about to cry, her nurse came in and announced that my mother needed to go down for a CAT scan. I sat in her hospital room alone, debating if I should leave. I called my dad.

"Dad," I sobbed. "I am at the hospital. She had a stroke. She is down for a CAT scan. I can't do this. I need to get out of here. I can't do this." My whole body was shaking.

"Try to breathe," my father said calmly. "Just breathe. You can leave whenever you want; you are in control. For now, just breathe."

I waited for my mother to come back up and asked her if she needed anything else before I left.

"You're leaving? You just got here."

"I can't stay, Mom. I left the kids with a sitter, and to be honest, I'm not interested in doing the same old routine with you. I didn't make the choice not to talk to you. You left my wedding, and I never once heard from you while Nicholas was sick. Not once. That was your choice!" I started to yell, and I was quickly getting angry. I knew I needed to leave—for me *and* for her. I let the tears flow down my face and I stared at her. "I love you, Mom. I have to go."

And she let me leave.

My mother was envious of me my whole life. Those words don't make sense to me as I write them, but there is no other way for me to explain why she never wanted me to be happy. Growing up with her emotional abuse, bad taste in men, drunken midnight arguments, and negligence the many times she ignored me, left scars so deep that even now, at 45 years old, I am still working out the trauma.

The most meaningful part of my healing process was when I started giving a voice to the child parts of me whose needs were not met; whose emotions had been blocked off. The little girl who felt neglected, confused, angry, anxious, panicked, baffled, hopeless, and depleted finally got to tell her story. I found that by allowing the 5-year-old me to talk about how anxious she felt just being around her mother, it freed up deeply buried emotions of conflict and confusion that I was feeling at 45. The work I did to unearth and uncover these emotions was raw and sometimes scary. But still, I let the 5-year-old speak about her feelings without applying any adult wisdom as to why she felt that way. It was an opportunity to allow my inner child to tell her story, without interruption.

For years in therapy, I made connections between the terrible things that happened to me and other people I helped, but I would layer over rational explanations as to why my mother, boyfriend, or anyone close to me would have acted as they had. I thought that understanding the why would help me release the pain. Analyzing her family life and perhaps understanding, for example, how my mother's parents treated her, would help me make sense of why she treated me the way she did. I used my wisdom and understanding to forgive her. Clearly, she didn't have the emotional tools to love and care for me.

But the little girl who was told she was a bad girl—the little girl who cried herself to sleep most nights—didn't care about wisdom and understanding, and she wasn't ready to forgive. She was scared, lost, and feeling like she wasn't loveable. And I needed to let her tell her story.

How often do you rationalize other people's actions?

Are you forgetting to also acknowledge how you feel about their actions?

We must not forget that in addition to understanding others, we must witness and understand ourselves as well. In fact, that should be our first priority.

Chapter 21
Conflict

*C*onflict and unpredictability are triggers for children of abusive parents. It's an emotional mess. Children love, fear, and hate their abuser, and they worry obsessively in times of unpredictability. The bad thing that *might* happen is always on their minds, and they try to control every detail in hope that they will be safe.

During the years of my mother's abuse, I hated her. As a young child, I would lay in my warm waterbed at night and dream about her dying. I wanted her gone. The part of me that hated my mother in order to survive had no tolerance for the Ashley who loved her on the rare occasion when she tucked me into bed and kissed me on the top of the head. The little girl whose main job was to ensure survival thought the one who would allow her mother to love us after such torment was pathetic and weak.

Not only was I receiving conflicting messages from my mother about her love for me, but I was split in two, conflicted about how I felt about her. The soft, loving, and quiet Ashley longed for her mother's love, and gracefully accepted it. Meanwhile the angry, protective Ashley was on high alert, knowing full well that she could not trust the woman we called mother. These two parts of me were at war with each other and fighting for my attention every single day.

I later learned that the human brain is not fully developed until age 25. So, when my young, impressionable, and still-growing brain was flooded with these huge emotions, it was too much for my nervous system, and thus, I would just shut down. I often wondered if I was hiding my emotions, or keeping them secret because I had not picked which one to feel. Because secrets cultivate unpredictability and mistrust, I was beginning not to trust my own feelings. Did I love her, or did I hate her? And which one was the secret?

When my mother got angry, she either tormented me or stopped talking to me. However, her feelings actually had nothing to do with me. When I began to heal, I came to understand that she was hiding her own buried and conflicted emotions and used my messy room, unaligned kitchen chairs, crumbs on the counter, or eye rolling as an excuse to treat me poorly so she could express her buried anger and frustration. I learned at a young age that when my mother became emotional, I was unsafe because I was her target.

My mother's behavior was also incredibly unpredictable, leaving me feeling uneasy most of my childhood. For years, I was sick while trying to control everything I could in my world, trying to make myself safe. Although it was not possible, I tried anyway.

Unpredictability and conflict are two things that I now work hard to live with as an adult. I still don't talk politics or religion at cocktail parties because topics this charged are unpredictable and almost always end in conflict. People's feelings often get hurt because you are asked to pick sides, and it emphasizes everyone's unhealed and buried emotions and internal conflict.

Even now, my body reacts and panics when I see conflict on TV, read social media arguments, or hear people arguing. I can pick up on the conflicted emotions of those who appear angry, and I can sense their unhealed wounds. I worry that they, like me, feel terrified. Conflict sits in my body like an inflatable pool you try to fold and fit back into its original box after using it for a few days. You might say I have a mainframe malfunction that vacillates between feelings of safe and unsafe, and the loop stays on repeat.

When my brain and body feel conflicted, I feel unsafe. It's hard-wired. When my husband doesn't show up for me when I am sick, the little girl whose job it is to protect me says that he can't be trusted. I also have a difficult time being upset with people I love because instinctually, I think I have to pick a side: love them or be mad at them. My brain doesn't know that I can love someone *and* be upset with them at the same time.

For years, I interpreted and filtered all situations in my marriage through the heart and eyes of my emotional other half, the abused little girl. She determined what was safe or not safe. There was no gray, just black and white. When Ari was withdrawn and angry because of work stress, I did two things. First, I jumped through hoops to make him happy. I made him his favorite dinner, told the kids to be extra quiet, offered him sex. You name it, I would do anything to make him happy to hold off the abuse my nervous system expected because of childhood. Because of my mother. If Ari was happy, I was safe.

Second, when Ari was angry or stressed, I began to panic. I would take on his anger like it was mine. I would feel it deep in my bones, and my body would respond with an increased heart rate, sour stomach, and anxiety. Triggered by Ari's anger, my body was being reminded of my mother. When she was angry, she hurt me. My brain naturally thought my husband would do the same.

So, did all this run through my head before it happened? No. It was all under the surface, unconscious behavior that my body resorted to in times of anxiety. It lived on in the parts of my brain where all the little, tiny Ashleys live. My body and brain waited, then panicked, then waited again. A few days later, Ari was inevitably fine and I was sick.

No wonder.

My body adapted to and thinks that it is normal to live with the stress hormones of cortisol and adrenaline that are a result of conflict and unpredictability. (I swear this is why I can't lose weight. My cortisol levels are still so high, preventing my hormones to regulate and begin to shed the extra weight.) Together, my brain and my body did whatever it had to do to help me survive during the years I lived with my mother, but it was stuck on that protective, anxious loop. I was caught between two poles: safe and unsafe.

Black and white thinking caused me to suffer as an adult because nothing is really black and white; no situation, person, or emotion. There is variability to life, a spectrum of emotions that will never fit into a black and white thinking pattern. Ari can love me and not see my hidden pain. This doesn't mean that when he fails to take care of me emotionally that I am unsafe. When we see the whole person or the whole situation, we are spectrum thinking, a full rainbow; not just black and white!

The situations of my childhood created a habit, a way of thinking that was hard for me to drop. Habits are difficult to change but not impossible; with a little hard work and faith the size of a mustard seed, changes can happen. During situations when those I love act in an unpredictable manner,

I have to work hard to remind my brain and body that I am not in danger; I am safe.

Conflict is everywhere. It is in our schools, our government, marriages, and relationships of all kinds. Conflict is never going away. According to dictionary.com, the definition of conflict is an incompatibility between two or more opinions, principles, or interests. For a lot of us, if we find ourselves incompatible with a mate, we leave. If we find food that's incompatible or inedible at a local restaurant, we don't go back.

But the truth is, incompatibility in and of itself isn't a bad thing. Differences are good. If we didn't have opposing views, what on God's green earth would we talk about? How boring would it be if we all looked the same and agreed about everything? What would musicians write songs about, and how would authors find material? How would we grow as a society, as humans? Opposing views makes for great conversations—if and *only* if we don't feel threatened. Fear inhibits tolerance, and when we have unresolved or conflicted emotions around the topic of discussion, we feel fear in the face of opposition. This is not only true for adults of childhood trauma, but for everyone else, too.

So, how do we move past feelings of being unsafe in the midst of conflict?

For me, it looked something like this: I went within and allowed myself to feel my feelings without judgment or repression. When feelings of anger, betrayal, or even shame bubbled to the surface, I talked about them. At first, I talked about them only in therapy; then as I got stronger, I talked about them with the person who triggered them. It was simple for me: just tell the person, "something came up for me the other day and I would like to share it with you."

Once I came to the realization that my triggers were about my feelings and not what the other person did or didn't do, I felt power in owning my stuff, and people were open to hearing it because they were not on the defensive. Shining light on shame is like sunlight to mold; it kills it. Our emotions fester if we ignore them, only growing more powerful. When we finally do talk about them, we find that they are much easier to manage.

Then, I built boundaries for my relationships. I made a list for every important person in my life detailing what I was and was not willing to do within the relationship. Once I was clear on what I wanted and was willing and not willing to do, it was easier to not jump when they called or walk away when they got angry over who was going to get elected President. I now filter all choices through what I decide is within my boundaries.

Boundaries are challenging to establish, but they feel so damn good once you have them. Having boundaries keeps me safe, allowing me to be with conflict and not feel panic, or think that the situation will bring on my physical symptoms. Boundaries are a non-negotiable to heal from trauma, and I recommend working with a trained therapist to begin this work.

The ability to hold two opposite emotions within my body has given me freedom from the incessant anxiety I felt when triggered. Knowing that I can be angry and frustrated with my husband and love him in the exact same moment was like winning the lottery. It takes more energy for me to fight with myself about having to make choices about how to handle arguments or marital ups and downs than it does to simply allow myself to feel the feelings. Doing this work has allowed me to truly know I am safe—all the time, no matter what.

Chapter 22
Observation

From the time we got home from the hospital with Nicholas, I had a knowing deep within me that I needed to release my past. My childhood trauma was creeping into my marriage, my work, and my relationships. So, I sought out healing modalities such as craniosacral body work, Reiki sessions with Lucinda, acupuncture, and many more. I would lay on their tables and pray silently to myself: "God, please give them the power to fix me. Please help them to take out of my body what is making me sick."

On top of going to healers, I tried kundalini yoga and meditation techniques taught by Dr. Joe Dispenza, listened to the work of Peter Crone, a motivational speaker who calls himself the mind architect, and Michael Singer, a *New York Times* best-selling author and meditation teacher. Each one of them (along with the many others I read or practiced with) provided the education to understand two important facts: the first was that my body had stored my past experiences in the form of energy. This energy was showing up as migraines and pain, and my thoughts associated with my past were making me sick. The second fact was that I had the power within me to let my past go—not ignore it, but rather simply not hold onto it like it was still currently happening. I knew if I changed my thoughts, my body would respond to a new me and a new reality of health and happiness.

Everyone I sought out talked about healing in a way that made sense to me. I was already tapped into the understanding that everything in us and around us is energy, and that there is a larger, more powerful energy of The Universe at work. I had spoken those same words and thoughts to many of my own clients. But for some reason, I was unable to translate the work I was reading and taking classes about into techniques for my *own* healing.

I mean, how do you just change your thoughts? I couldn't understand it. Remember, situations appear to be simple, black and white math to me, like 2+2=4. If my husband leaves me when I am at my lowest, that equals four. He doesn't love me. If Nicholas got cancer and Evi died, that also equals four. Bad things happen to my family. If I don't know what is going to happen next, and I can't control the current situation, that equals four. I am not safe. See? Simple math.

During these months when I was focused on my theory that my past was predicting my future, I heard Pedro in my head telling me, "Your anxiety is making you sick." I felt an immense pressure on myself to make it right; to fix my thinking. I wanted to let go of my past, but I simply didn't know how. Once I admitted to myself (and to Ari) how anxious I truly was on a daily basis, I began to see how my symptoms of headaches and dizziness almost always followed a scary thought or stressful situation.

I can say without a doubt that if I had not been meditating as regularly as I was at the time, it would have taken me much longer to see the connection between my thoughts and symptoms. My meditations were giving me the ability to observe myself during the day, rather than being so stuck in the weeds of each moment that I couldn't see what my triggers were.

Observation is key to making meaningful change, as we can't change what we don't see. What I *could* see most prevalently in 2019 was how angry at myself I was, how pathetic I saw myself for being sick. The way I would talk to myself was downright disgusting, and that was just the start of it.

Oftentimes, I would open my eyes in the morning and within the very first few moments of my day I would notice that I had a migraine. Many chronic migraineurs have first-thing-in-the-morning headaches. They are awful, and it can ruin a day you were looking forward to. In fact, the mere pressure of looking forward to the day of activities and family time ahead was too much for my nervous system, and that stress alone would trigger a migraine. I felt incredibly deflated, and depressed, really. Another migraine; another day ruined.

On those days, after brushing my teeth, I'd stare at myself in the mirror as if I was looking for someone inside me that I recognized. "Fucking pull yourself together," I'd say. "Stop this bullshit of another migraine. There is nothing about today that you need to be so anxious for. There is no reason to have this much anxiety, and today doesn't have to be a headache day. Cut the shit. You are so pathetic." Then I would saunter downstairs, make the kids breakfast, kiss them goodbye for school, and then cry as soon as I heard the garage door close. I was trying so hard to be a good wife and mother, and I felt like I was failing every day.

Meanwhile, my thoughts were on autopilot. *Another headache; another day ruined. This will never end.* I hid how anxious and angry I was, but simply stuffing down those emotions was like trying to fit a comforter into a trash bag, and I was repeating the same old behavior of my past—ignoring my emotions.

Why was I so anxious and unkind to myself? Where did this talk come from? Why would I speak to myself so poorly? How was I able to walk around in so much physical and emotional pain while people around me barely noticed?

All of these answers came to me through inner child work. Once I started, I began to see patterns of thinking that led back to my childhood, and these thought loops were signaling my body that I was unsafe. A mere thought and I was back in my mother's house enduring her abuse all over again. A smell could send me back into our days in the hospital, or the way the sunlight hit the walls in the evening would remind me of when I was at my lowest and bedridden. Finally being able to observe that it was the smell or the angle of the sunlight that triggered my anxiety was such a gift in my healing journey. It gave me answers because not knowing where the anxiety came from, and feeling like it just appeared out of nowhere, always made it feel more intense and scary.

From there, I was able to connect that the anxiety was about a buried emotion, and the smell told me to explore my time in the hospital with Nicholas. If it was the sunlight, I would sit and ask myself, "What am I feeling right now that is connected to the time when I was bedridden?" Being able to observe myself like this allowed me to take the next step—the uncovering.

Having compassion for ourselves is how we learn to have tolerance for others. My husband couldn't bear to see me so broken and ill because I think it scared him that one day he might be that fragile. If he allowed himself to see and accept me as fragile, it meant he would have to accept within himself that it was a possibility for him. Those were emotions that were never packed in his survival backpack. He didn't have access to the feelings of self-compassion; he always had to be perfect, strong, and unbreakable. So, naturally, it didn't come easy for him to hold that space for me.

Ari and I share so many of the same traits. I always hated weakness in others. I found it boring and took little time with those I perceived as weak. This was because I never allowed *myself* to be weak. I took the abuse of my mother and used it as fuel to be self-sufficient. I used the terror of Nicholas to start a charity. I never allowed the struggle to break me. Many people would describe me as strong and say that I am unbreakable. However, my strength has only gotten deeper as I've allowed myself some compassion. I now know that hating myself for any kind of failure and belittling myself when I was struggling to live with chronic pain was what kept me sick. In my life, the struggle didn't mean that I was being strong; it meant I was being an asshole to myself.

Today, through my journaling, I have learned to bathe in my emotions rather than run from them. When a particular feeling arises that is causing me physical pain, I allow the little girl who is triggered into thinking we are living in the past to come forward and talk. Every single time I do this, I am fascinated by what comes up. The changes I have made are not only positively affecting me and my marriage, but I am changing family patterns of behavior passed down generation to generation. I let my inner child talk to me through my writing, and it often looks like this:

Dear Things Have to Be Perfect,

We must keep the house tidy and line up the chairs. She is coming home soon; we need to be ready. Are there crumbs on the counter? You remember what happened last time we left those—she woke us up in the middle of the night to clean them up. That sucked. What about the carpet in the living room, did we re-vacuum the lines? She will know we sat on that couch if there are feet marks on the carpet. Did we vacuum??? Hurry, vacuum, hurry.

> *After all, healing is a process, not a goal*

Take a quick look in the bathroom, too. Anything amiss? Better double check, she will be home soon. Oh god, she just pulled in, I can see her lights. Hurry, run into your room and be quiet. Do homework, be quiet. SSSH, here she comes. Oh God, she slammed the door, I can tell that slam; she is mad.

Aah, makes sense then that our house today must be perfect. I get it now, why I flip out when my kids leave their stuff everywhere and the house seems messy. I see why crumbs on the counter make me so angry. I am freaking out because my brain is telling me I am in trouble. Thank you little Ashley; thank you for this story.

Let me tell you this: we are safe today. Crumbs are OK, and the kids' stuff is actually a good thing; we have happy healthy kids! Yah!! We can leave the house a little messy and we won't get into trouble, not anymore. We are safe, hear me say this… we are safe!

Life isn't perfect, and neither is healing. I go through ups and downs like everyone else. What is important here is that more than 80 percent of the time, I can catch my pain before it gets out of control. The other 20 percent of the time, I fall apart. I cry, I sleep, and I journal. It is these times that little Ashley is doing her best to be heard. She is trying to tell me something that I need to let go of because she is trying to heal. I simply have to be open and let her talk.

After all, healing is a process, not a goal.

Can you see yourself in this chapter?

Can you identify a child part of you who might be crying out for help or to be heard?

I encourage you to sit down and ask yourself if there's any emotion that wants to come up and if it is attached to childhood.

You can use this journal entry as an example and talk to this part of you and make sure they are heard.

Chapter 23
Ghosts

While Nicholas was in the hospital getting his cancer treatment, I started in vitro fertilization (IVF). Nicholas needed a bone marrow transplant, and at the time, Boston Children's believed that a matched sibling was the best donor for a successful transplant. Ari and I knew we eventually wanted to have more children, which made the decision to start IVF easier. Our plan was to give Nicholas a 50/50 genetic match and have our second child at the same time.

I found an IVF doctor close by and pushed my way into getting an appointment. When I first called, they tried to schedule me a month out. "Oh, that wasn't going to work," I cried. "My son has cancer, and I need to see the doctor tomorrow."

At my initial appointment, the doctor tried to convince me that what I was doing wasn't a good idea. "Where will it stop for *this* child? What if Nicholas needs further transplants or more therapy that only his sibling can provide?" he flatly asked us. "How fair will it be for them? Have you read *My Sister's Keeper* by Jodi Picoult?"

I had, and I firmly answered back. "Doc, do you have kids? If one of them was in a car accident and needed an organ transplant, and it turns out that one of your other children was a perfect match for the best results, would you deny your first child this life saving surgery? I don't think you would. I know this is going to be difficult going forward, and we will do our very best to consider both children down the line, but right now I need to save my son."

I started IVF the next day.

On my way back to the hospital from my first appointment, I was desperate to talk to my mother. More like I was desperate for *a* mother, but I decided to reach out to mine anyway. It had been almost seven months since she and I talked; seven months since Nicholas was born. I dialed her number, and when she answered, I immediately started to cry.

"Mom?" I choked.

"What is it, Ashley? What's wrong?"

"Nicholas is sick, he has cancer."

"Do you want me to come home?"

"NO!! Don't come," I screamed, likely too loudly. She was silent. Shit, she is mad at me now. Fuck.

"Mom, listen, the hospital only lets two people in at a time, and the room is tiny. Where would you stay? It's too much. Let me get settled in and we can go from there, OK?"

"Fine," she said, almost whispering. "When did this happen?" she asked.

"May."

"May? It is July. Why are you just telling me now?"

This is not how I saw this conversation going in my head. I was hoping for "Oh honey, I am so sorry. What can I do for you?" or "Oh my god, are you OK?" Instead, we argued about why I didn't call her first, and that I wasn't "letting" her come home. We struggled through the conversation, and it ended with my giving her as much information as I knew about Nicholas's cancer. I gave her the link to my daily blog and told her that she could get updates there. After we hung up, I cried the entire drive back to Children's. I felt abandoned and alone, yet *again*.

The following week, Nicholas became very ill. His blood counts were zero, and he needed several blood transfusions a day just to stay alive. He was bleeding internally, but we didn't know from where or why. Chemotherapy kills cancer cells, but it also kills healthy cells, including white and red blood cells. Because his blood counts were so low at this point due to the chemo, the doctors were guessing as to why he was so sick and nearing death's door. The theory was that the chemo had made a slight tear in his bowel because he was pooping blood all day.

When you are a healthy individual and you bleed, your body mounts a response and sends white blood cells to the area to try to clot the blood. In Nicholas's case, he didn't have any red or white blood cells because the chemo had killed off everything, and his body was not able to send white blood cells to the area of bleeding like a healthy child could. To make matters worse, he was having severe allergic reactions to these transfusions, but they were keeping him alive.

He also had really high fevers, and we all suspected an infection on top of the bleeding of some kind. Cancer patients, especially those who live in the hospital, are prone to infections. Nicholas had already had over six staph infections. The medical team was concerned about his fragility and wanted him to move to the ICU so they could monitor him constantly. I was fighting that move because the little boy on the floor who left the previous week to go to the ICU never came back. I was so afraid of Nicholas dying. Ultimately, Nicholas coded, which meant the decision to be in the ICU was made for us.

I'll never forget it—alarms went off by his bedside and in a nanosecond, there were eight doctors in our tiny room. I was in the crib with him when they asked me to leave.

"Mom, we need you to step aside so we can save your son," one of the young-looking doctors from the ICU said.

I told them there wasn't a chance in hell that I was leaving Nicholas and to work around me. I held onto his tiny feet, telling him over and over, "Stay with me, Nicholas, stay with Mommy." I was barely breathing, subconsciously holding my breath.

He made it through, and we moved onto the ICU floor. Each day we spent there we focused on getting his body to accept the blood transfusions by dosing him with Benadryl and other antihistamines. Our goal was to keep him from going into anaphylactic shock while also trying to figure out where he was bleeding internally.

I posted two or three times a day on my blog during the time Nicholas was in the ICU, giving people both the medical update as well as an update on our emotional state as a family. I was honest and raw, leaving everything I had on those pages. The day we moved to the ICU, I asked everyone to pray for Nicholas to make it through the night. I was honest about my fear of him dying. In the backend of this blog site, I could see who logged on and when. My mother had signed up for updates right after our call, and she logged in and read every single one. She read the post about moving to the ICU; she read the post where her daughter poured her heart out begging God to save her son.

But she didn't reach out to me once during that trip to the ICU. She didn't even reach out once while we were in the hospital at all. In fact, I never spoke with her again until she had her stroke. It was more than 10 years before I uttered the word "Mom" to her again. This is why ultimately, I left her in the hospital room the day she had her stroke. It is why I told her no when she asked to live with me. She never called me while Nicholas was ill—not even once. And I *never* forgot how it felt.

I was numb with fear while Nicholas was in the hospital. There was no time to feel anything else. My mother not showing up for me only added to the numbness and reinforced the protective wall I had built for both Nicholas and me. Talking about this in therapy was too painful, so I stopped. My plan was to move forward and let go of those haunting times. As the years passed and Nicholas remained healthy, I tried to put the past behind me, and I chose to put all my energy into One Mission. I figured I would heal with time. But I didn't understand that healing can't take place when you are ignoring what happened. The running and working and not feeling as a coping mechanism wasn't helping me, as I had hoped, but was actually hurting me.

If you know you need to heal, putting it off for a better day doesn't work. Rather than acknowledging the worry about Nicholas's health, I became hyper-focused on the charity getting bigger and even more successful. I worked 15-hour days to keep my focus on something other than the trauma I had endured.

I stopped talking about my mother, too. She was dead to me. I let her go.

But that was a mistake. Not only was it detrimental for my healing to not talk about Nicholas's treatment, but it was a crucial mistake to once again not give voice to the little girl who was devastated by her mother's betrayal. She needed to speak about her pain. We cannot hide from our emotions for long. They are like ghosts in the closet.

They come out when you least expect them to.

Chapter 24
Saying Goodbye

The stroke that my mother had was caused by tumors in her brain—she had cancer. After her stroke, we were trying to mend our relationship. Actually, I was trying. She didn't change at all.

My mother had not met any of my three beautiful, kind, and loving children and there was no way in hell that I was going to bring her into their lives until we were on stable ground. That was my goal, to get us in a good place—a place where we could get along, being kind and loving to one another. I couldn't risk her treating my children the way she treated me. I didn't want that for them. Unfortunately, it never happened.

In the same breath she told me that she had cancer, she also told me that she had decided to forgo any treatment. She said that after watching others go through cancer treatment, she didn't want to poison her body that same way. She just wanted to let her body die naturally. My mother wanted to die, to give up on life without ever fixing things between us.

I flipped out. Completely lost it. We were finally talking again after almost 15 years, and she was giving up.

"So that's it?" I said. "You're just not even going to fight, you just want to die?" I was having a total body experience of sheer anger as we talked on the phone.

"Yep," she replied, without one ounce of empathy for the fact that I was losing my mother all over again. It was summer, and I was arguing in my backyard on Cape Cod. My neighbors could hear everything I was screaming because our houses were so close together. I chose to have my neighbors hear my cries rather than my small children inside the house.

"Fuck you!" I screamed. "Fuck you for every single day you tortured me, left me, and hurt me. Fuck you for dumping this stroke and now cancer on me only to leave me all over again. I want nothing to do with you if you don't choose to fight. Fight for yourself, and fight for me," I was shaking. In the same breath, I hung up on her.

Our phone call happened minutes before I had to walk into a One Mission fundraising event. I was dressed and ready, makeup on, and my employees were waiting for me in the car. After I hung up, I dropped my phone on the grass and screamed bloody murder at the top of my lungs. Then I wiped the tears from my cheeks, blew my nose, and got in the car and drove us to the marina where our charity's fishing tournament was taking place.

It was impossible for me to keep my composure. I was so upset I couldn't even talk without crying. I had to pinch myself in the bathroom and run cold water over my wrists right before I was to give the welcome speech, trying to snap myself out of the melodrama that I had been sucked back into with her. All that was running through my head as I sold raffle tickets and thanked people for their donations was, "I can't believe that this is my life; that I am back in her web of manipulation. I feel like I'm 10 all over again." I felt trapped.

Late that fall, as I drove my kids home from school one day, I wondered what would have happened if I never went to see her after Joan called me. What would have happened if I chose myself back then, rather than feeling guilty about leaving her in her hospital room alone? Should I have let her remain already dead to me?

Almost a month later, I heard from her again. She decided to try treatment. I was shocked. Was she choosing me after all this time? I figured we would work things out over those months of chemo, and I felt hopeful that we would find common ground. Cancer does that to people. Facing death's door can put things in perspective for people. I was truly hoping that our relationship was going to turn the corner—that she would own her part; tell me that she loved me, and despite how she treated me, I would forgive her and we would start fresh.

It didn't happen like that. She started treatment that fall and continued into the late winter. Early on in her first or second round of chemo, she asked me for money. She couldn't pay her rent because she wasn't working, and she didn't have enough money to turn her heat on. I sent her wool hats for her bald head, blankets, and money. We had been talking off and on for a few months when she asked me for the first time if she could come and live with me.

My mother wanted to live with me... in *my* home with *my* husband and children. The woman who, time and time again, chose so many other things before me: boyfriends, booze, and friends, but usually just herself. Did she think I forgot? I was speechless. She actually thought we were in a place in our relationship where she could come and live with me and I would take care of her. After all we had been through.

The guilt and burden of the situation was eating me up. I didn't want her in my home, and I certainly didn't want to take care of her. I told her I would ask Ari, but I never did. A week later, I told her that I couldn't do it. I tried to explain to her that my wounds were still too raw; that I couldn't make that sacrifice and put my family through her living with us as sick as she was. I needed to put my three children and husband first. I told her that when she got better, I would bring her into my life slowly as we healed.

I never heard from her again. I called and left messages without receiving any reply. The following weeks were deeply unsettling for me. I was back in the same headspace of fear and anxiety and worry that my mother was mad at me, obsessing about why she cut me off again.

It was on a cold, wintry day that my mother's brother, Steve, called to tell me that my mother was at the end of her life. He moved her into a nursing home in Connecticut near where he lived. He wanted her close to him so he could visit her daily. He knew I would not.

I had made it to the end of the road with my mother, and now, this was it. She was dying. And we were not talking, yet again. For a week, I stayed up and stared at the wall, pacing my house in the dark of night trying to decide if I should go and see her before she died. My uncle called every few days to give me updates, which just made it worse for me. He was reminding me of the decision I had to make.

I was a zombie, not sleeping and drinking too much caffeine. One day, I was at my desk staring at a PowerPoint presentation I had made for a pitch on behalf of One Mission. I was drinking my coffee when it hit me—I needed to drive to Connecticut to see my mother. So, I got in the car and headed down. I was filling my car with gas when my father called me.

"Hi, Peach, just checking in on you. What are you up to?"

"I'm on my way to see my mother, getting gas now," I said.

"Are you alone? You can't go alone."

"I will be fine, Dad. Don't worry."

"Ashley, you are not driving alone to go and say goodbye to your mother. Pick me up; I'll drive with you." So, I did. We drove together, both in reflective silence. Having my dad next to me gave me all the support I needed.

The roads were quiet, barren of life, and had the silence of winter. The drive was pretty in a weird sort of way. I was thinking hard about what I was going to say to her. Would she even know I was there? I had been at the deathbeds of so many others. I knew what I was walking into—the smell, the sounds of the hollow body and erratic breathing. I just wasn't prepared for it to be my mother.

It really hit me when I walked in. My mother's nearly lifeless body lay in the hospital bed. She was bald, no more than 80 pounds, and she was alone. I was uncomfortable and overwhelmed with the influx of emotions. My head and my body instantly became overheated, like the feeling you get right before you throw up. All I wanted to do was run out of there as fast as I could.

The nursing home grounds looked calm as the snow began to cover the grass. I longed to be on the other side of the window in the fresh falling snow. I needed air. I stood at the window for a long time before I could sit by her side. I just stared at her, shaking inside and out. Then the emotions started to come up without my permission. I instinctively bit my lip and quickly tasted blood. I didn't want to cry. I was afraid if I started to cry, I would never stop—that I'd lose control and the nursing staff would have to sedate me. I was afraid of everything I was thinking and feeling; it was all coming in so fast. My mother was dying.

I left the window and stood at the edge of her bed.

"So, I am here," I said. "Not sure what else to say to you at this point. I want to tell you that I love you." A nurse walked in, as if on cue. She could see me crying and quickly turned on her heels and walked out. I used that as a sign to continue talking.

"I will never know why you chose not to come home some nights when I was in high school. I will never know why you banished me to my room when you had boyfriends over. I will never know why you thought it was a good idea to date a boy I went to high school with. I will never know why you didn't come to my graduation, or why you left my wedding. I will never know why you logged on to every one of my blog posts when Nicholas was in the hospital, but you didn't reach out to me once to check on me. I will never know this, Mother, because now you are dying. You are leaving me for the last time." My voice was calm and low, barely audible. "You ruined my life," I told her, and walked out into the hallway. I ran into my uncle Steve, who was waiting for me there. We didn't talk about the tears rolling down my face. I just gave him a hug and he invited me back into the room to sit with him.

We returned to her room and sat at her bedside together for an hour, and began talking.

"What happened between you two, anyway?" he asked me. My mother lay between us as we sat in the green plastic hospital chairs. I took a deep breath and told him everything. I started when I was five after my parents' divorce; I told him that on those Sundays when my father would drop me off, I would come home to find my mother laying in the dark on the living room floor listening to music.

"It was only once that I interrupted her," I told him. "Only once that I ran to her side thinking that she was dead. I only made that mistake once because she screamed at me to leave her alone. I was five."

I told him my story all the way up to my wedding night, and then I paused. "What did she tell you?" I asked him, truly terrified of what his answer was going to be.

"She told all of us that you asked her to leave your wedding," he said, "and then she made us promise not to talk to you. She told us that you didn't want her in your life, and you made that clear to her. We wanted to support her, so we cut you off too."

I had spent so many hours in therapy trying to figure out what was going through my mother's head, trying to figure out the story she was telling herself all those years. That was exactly what my therapist and I conjured up—that she was lying to everyone to make herself look like the victim. We were right, but in this moment, it didn't feel good to be right.

My mother was lying about me to her *family*. That shouldn't have surprised me as much as it did, because I watched her lie to everyone my whole life about our relationship. She made it seem like I was a girl who just walked away from her mother, cutting her out of my life, and for what? Why would I do that?

Now the truth was out, and there was no more guessing about my mother's state of mind during my life. I knew. She chose to walk away from me, she chose not to show up for me when my son had cancer, and she chose to not make things work to meet my daughters. My mother did not choose me.

I'd had enough, and it was time for me to go. I was numb. My mother was making the loud moaning and breathing noises that people do at the end of their life. I stood up and told my uncle that, in my experience, my mother had a few more days before she died. I could tell by her breathing pattern. I left with no plans to return. I finally had the truth, and I didn't think I had any reason to come back to see her.

Almost a week had gone by when my uncle called to tell me that the nurses thought my mother would pass in the next 24 hours.

After I hung up, I just stood in my bathroom staring at myself in the mirror. The older I got, the more I looked like my mother. I looked at every wrinkle, glaring at my nose and mouth. I was searching for answers. Do I let my mother die alone?

I got the kids off to school and went home to sit in meditation for a while and ask God for help. "Dear God, what should I do? Do I sit with my mother as she takes her last breath, or do I let her die alone? What will help me best in the end? I don't want to regret my decision. I need peace," I said. "I just want to feel peace."

I put on my Deepak meditation CD, but I must have fallen asleep when it was done. Hours had passed by the time I opened my eyes.

I knew what I was supposed to do. So I put my shoes on and drove to Connecticut.

The nurses were right. I could tell that she was at the very end. But there was something off, and I could tell she was holding on. There was a part of her that was fighting inside. I brought a few of the crystals I use during meditation; rose quartz for healing the heart, and amethyst for healing pretty much anything. I placed the crystals around her body and put a small healing card with Jesus on her bedside table. I picked up her hand and held onto it.

"Mom, I want you to go home in peace," I said. "I will be OK. I forgive you for how you treated me, and I forgive you for lying. I know that we will be together again in another lifetime, and maybe then we will get it right." I moved my right hand to her heart and placed my left hand on her forehead, hand positions that I had done so many times with my clients. I took in a deep breath and said, "I call upon my mother's spirit guides and angels. Please come and take her home. Bless her body and spirit, she is free now to leave us here. To leave me here. I am ready to let her go. I ask you all to stay with her and to love her as she moves on into heaven. Amen."

I kissed her on the head and walked out of her room shaking. She died a few hours later.

Wanting to forgive someone and actually releasing the energy between you isn't always simple. I held onto a bit of anger for a few years (actually a lot of years) after my mother died. My mind understood all of it—who she was, why she acted the way she did. The wisdom in me understood and was ready to let go. However, the child part of me was nowhere ready, and it wasn't until I let her tell her story that I finally began to release my mother. I wish I could have done it all at once, like ripping off a Band-Aid that has been stuck on you for too long. Fast. But healing your inner child does not work that way. I had to go slowly and methodically, chapter by chapter through my life.

Early on, before the migraines, there were many times that my mother would try to come into my meditations or energy healing sessions. The energy workers would say, "Your mother is here, and she wants to talk." I would reply the same way each time: "No, tell her to go away."

It wasn't until I was living in Rhode Island while getting treatment with Pedro that I let my mother into my energy field.

It was a particularly bad night of symptoms, and I was sick, dizzy, crying, and scared. I was praying for God to help me. My mother's face came right in and I could smell her perfume. And I let her in. I said out loud, "If you are here to help me, then I will let you stay, but that is all I want you to do tonight. Help me feel better. I need help, Mom, please help me to get better."

I allowed myself to drift back into the vertigo, free falling, and when I did, I envisioned my mother and her mother taking care of me in my mind's eye. It was like the movies I had seen so many times in my life, playing before me in the darkness of my closed eyes. My grandmother Lois was in her old school white nursing uniform with the white hat and white sneakers. She was laying her hands on my head, and my mother stood behind her.

My mother was not a healer like her mother was. It came to me like a knowing: my mother didn't have the power or the tools necessary for the work, so she had brought me her mother in order to heal me that night. It was a beautiful gesture, one that I thanked my mother for profusely the next morning as I recalled the episode. Shortly after I allowed my grandmother take care of me, I finally fell asleep.

By letting my mother in like this, I opened the door to healing our wound. I was opening my heart to her in a way I never had while she was alive. Slowly but surely, I started forgiving my mother bit by bit. I know that she was a sick woman who loved me as best she could. Her best was awful, but it was still her best. I do the work to release her and her unhealthy patterns of behavior for my own children because I love them with every ounce of my being.

The past doesn't simply disappear. Remember: words, actions, and emotions are all energy that stays within families, passed on like the Christmas china. Trauma can repeat throughout generations, too, because it is a learned response of behavior; it's ancestral. I am healing myself to stop my family's cycle of neglect and abuse. I am healing so my children heal and their children do, too. The buck stops here.

I have vowed that the patterns of abuse and neglect stop with me. I may not be a perfect parent, but I will never hold back love from any of my children as a way to punish or hurt them. I am open and honest with my children when I am struggling. I own when I am wrong, and I apologize often. Hallelujah!

What would my life be like today if my mother had done any of those things just once? Just once…

Chapter 25
Hope

I started working with a pain coach named Anna in March of 2020 after having read her blog post about chronic pain. The article was sent to me by the Curable app I was using for my migraines, which I had found one day while scrolling through Facebook. You know how it works, you Google "Why am I getting daily migraines" and then all of a sudden, your Facebook feed is chock full of migraine medication advertisements. Lucky for me, one of the ads was for the Curable app.

Curable changed my life. It provided me with an education on chronic pain that I had never heard before. It also gave real-time techniques to bring down my pain level during an attack. By using the techniques in the app, I was able to function with my migraines; I was able to pick the kids up at school again, attend work meetings, and eat dinner with my family. My anxiety was still incredibly high, but my pain level began hovering around 7 on a scale of 1-10 (10 being the worst). To put this in perspective, I had been living at level 12 (off the scale) for as long as I could remember.

Slowly but surely, my daily headaches were becoming livable. If I felt a migraine coming on, I would put on my headphones and plug into the app, following the guided meditations it provided. Almost every time I used the app, my pain level would go from 12 or more down to 5 or 6. Every time.

Curable has a host of medical doctors and therapists who are a part of their consortium that helps their followers heal from chronic pain. Anna is one of them. The title of her article stopped me dead in my tracks: "6 Steps for Getting Out of a Panic Spiral."

Here is an excerpt:

> Chronic pain and anxiety tend to go hand in hand. Dr. John Sarno links the two in his book *The Divided Mind*, and when I first came across his work through the Curable app, it immediately made sense. As a long-time migraine sufferer, my most common headache trigger is what I call "the panic spiral."

> Maybe you know what I'm talking about. The panic spiral is like a traffic jam of anxiety triggers in your mind. It might start with an overwhelming to-do list of family obligations that collides with a seemingly insurmountable pile of paperwork from your boss and… do you feel what's happening in your body just reading this? The panic spiral can hamstring your logical reasoning, limit your sense of what's possible, and even bring on physical constriction and pain.

I sent Anna an email immediately after reading her article. I felt in my bones that this was how I was going to heal. My first session with Anna was different than any other therapy sessions I had ever had. As I often had with other therapists, I began to tell Anna my life story, trying to fit in all the pertinent details into our 50 minutes together.

"What brings you to me, Ashley? Tell me what is going on," she asked.

"Well, let's see, my parents got divorced when I was five, my mother was emotionally abusive to me. High school was torture, and my son had cancer when he was a baby. I have chronic migraines, and my life is a mess because of them," I blurted out. I took a breath, ready to go on.

"Would it be OK if I stopped you?" she said softly.

"Oh, um sure."

Anna explained that the way we were going to work together differed a little from previous therapies I had experienced. She told me that my chronic migraines were most likely rooted in deep anxiety and fear that had come from past trauma. Anna went on to explain that those who suffer from chronic pain have sensitive nervous systems, and it was likely that trauma after trauma was what sent my nervous system into overdrive, forcing the thought that a current situation was unsafe even though the true threat was not present today.

She asked if we could start today with a simple question: "How are you feeling today, Ashley?" She paused and waited for me to wipe the tears from my face. I already felt so safe with her.

"I have the worst headache; I can't take it anymore," I cried. "I just need to be better. I am not a good mother when I am in pain. I can barely sit and talk with my husband, my marriage is falling apart, I am not working, and I am so overwhelmed with all of it."

Anna gently guided me through a relaxation exercise and helped me to calm my body down. Then she asked me to find the loudest emotion within me.

"I am so worried," I said. In her soft voice, Anna asked me to share what it was that I was worried about.

"What if I never get better? What if I am sick like this for the rest of my life?" I cried.

"What are you worried will happen if you are sick like this forever?" she asked.

I began to explain to her the worries that were circling my head: "My marriage will end in divorce for sure. The kids will need me, and I won't be able to show up for them. These migraines are ruining my life."

Calmly, Anna said, "Let's break it down. Tell me why your marriage will end if you are sick."

"Because Ari needs me to be there for him, to take care of him, have sex, go out for dinner, all those things. When I am sick, I can't do any of that."

"So, what you're saying is that you think Ari won't accept you if you stay sick. Can we explore perhaps some other times in your life when you were not accepted? Can you tell me about those, Ashley?" Anna's words felt like a warm fuzzy blanket, wrapping me in comfort and safety.

"Oh, my mother never accepted me. We had a terrible relationship up to her last breath."

"Let's start the work here. I think this is a good place to explore."

From there, Anna had me make a list of emotions I identified with using a list found on the Center for Nonviolent Communication (CNVC) website (https://www.cnvc.org/about). This global organization supports the learning and sharing of Nonviolent Communication (NVC) and helps people peacefully and effectively resolve conflicts in personal, organizational, and political settings.

She read through the list and paused at each emotion, waiting for my answer. My list was long: anxious, embarrassed, panicked, scared, worried, exasperated… it went on and on.

"Would you be open to an exercise of inviting all of the parts of you to come and sit in a circle?"

I had no idea what she was talking about, but I agreed to be open. I closed my eyes and took a deep breath.

"Picture yourself in the room you are in, and that you are at the head of the circle. Let's ask the little girl who is embarrassed to come forward. Ask her to join our circle. Can you see her?" she asked.

I nodded my head. "Good, let's continue."

By the end of this visualization, I had 33 little girls, little Ashleys in my circle.

"Now, tell them, in your own words, that you are here to listen to them. Tell them that you know they all have a story to tell you. It will take time, but you will get to each and every one of them."

As soon as I started the exercise, I began sobbing. "I see every one of you," I said. "I want to hear what you have to tell me. Your story is important to me, and I promise to listen. Please be patient with me. It may take a while, but I won't walk away from you. We are in this together. I love you all." I opened my eyes, and my face was covered with tears.

"How are you feeling right now?" she asked.

"Like I lost 50 pounds," I said, and I just kept crying.

"Good, that is good. I want you to take some time this weekend to journal. Invite the little girl who is anxious to come forward and tell you how she is feeling. Her story will help us to untangle your chronic pain. Don't use the wisdom of the 45-year-old you, just let the little girl parts of you come forward," she instructed.

I did as I was told. The very next day, I journaled after my morning mediation and have journaled this way every day since then. After my first session with Anna, I didn't get another headache for over 40 days. That was the longest I had gone without pain in almost two whole years. I was convinced that this was going to work. Working with Anna was going to bring me freedom from pain.

I was full of hope.

Anna emailed me the list of emotions and needs from the non-violent communication source she used during our exercise, and I used it as a guide when I first began to journal because it was difficult for me to access the emotions I had spent years burying. I really had no idea what I was doing at first, but I just went with it. I added journaling to my already established morning routine of praying and meditating.

There were many days I would start off writing the words "I don't know what to write about today," or "I hate journaling." Even those prompts elicited a response. I would begin, "I have no idea what to write about today," then it would start to pour out. "I mean I could write about how fucking mad I am that I have to do this journaling, but that is stupid. This whole thing is stupid. It is weak and pathetic that I even need to talk about all the shit from childhood. I am so annoyed and mad that it even happened, and even more annoyed at myself for letting my past have any effect on my present life. It is over, gone, done, why do I even care?"

After I finished an entry, I would go back and circle all of the emotions that ran like thread through my entry. Annoyed, pathetic, angry, frustrated. Immediately after I would start again with:

"Dear Annoyed…" and I would let the little girl who was so annoyed with her mother go on about whatever it is she needed to tell me she was so annoyed about. It fascinated me to see all that I kept buried inside. I was annoyed with my mother as a teenager and young adult. But what really struck me was that I was also annoyed with myself then, too—for many things. The connection I made to moments in my present life when I felt annoyed, and how it connected back to the buried emotion of annoyed from my past, allowed me to understand that my brain could not decipher the difference between past event and present situation. I continued to make connections like this for months, and I still do.

Chronic pain, trauma, and anxiety go hand in hand. Over the years, I have met with many chronic pain patients, and through talking to them, I saw that we all shared the chronic anxiety piece as well. And we all had the anxiety before the pain. Healing is a process that takes dedication and patience, but uncovering our true selves is worth every tear and uncomfortable emotion we experience. I like myself more now than I ever have, and journaling helped me to see my true colors. I am a rainbow filled with emotions that flow up and through me; I am more than just black and white.

———————————

If this type of work is resonating with you, I have a free meditation on my website called "Meeting of the Children."

I encourage you to check it out and spend some time meeting with the child parts of you who want to come forth!

———————————

Chapter 26
Authenticity

*B*eing authentic to our true self takes courage in today's world. It requires stepping over the judgments of others, our own self judgments, and untangling the perceptions and labels learned and placed upon us during childhood. To be authentic is to truly be who we are at a soul level, in the form in which we were brought to earth. Our authentic self is the energy, the soul, that resides in our human body. Being authentic should be far easier than putting on a façade, or a fake persona. Unfortunately, as children, many of us were programmed into thinking that who we are isn't good enough. Every single event, conversation and interaction we have as children encourages us into trying to become someone else; someone we think that the world will like better.

It starts at a young age and can be seemingly benign: *Good girls don't speak up, and strong boys don't cry.* This never-ending societal programming establishes roots in childhood that act as the foundation to our belief system in our adult lives. Indeed, a young girl who was told over and over to be less assertive and quiet will grow into a woman who cannot say no, or won't speak up when sexually harassed in her workplace.

This is tragic because many girls are actually born to be vocal, to speak up and make waves. I was born to lead, to teach, and to create change within my life and the lives of those around me. I felt this at a young age, but it took me until my 40s to be able to truly step into my power.

In my opinion, my mother never heard the calling back to her soul, and thus never lived an authentic life. How was she programmed as she grew up? I don't know. Perhaps the lifestyle of her parents as they worked opposite shifts programmed her to not need the connection of loved ones, or to not trust it if she were to ever get it. Her father seemed a little standoffish even to me as a child, so perhaps that lack of connection hindered her ability to express her own love. Maybe not being openly shown love is why she had a difficult time connecting to me as a mother herself.

I liken life and our perception of what is good, bad, and what feels good to a pair of glasses. We all have a pair of these glasses whose frames are aesthetically pleasing to us but whose glass is made up of tiny broken fragments. These broken fragments are our experiences of pain and suffering; our scars. As adults, we make decisions through these glasses. They act like a filter through which we funnel opinions on everything from work, family, and love, to our self-worth and value. The broken lens, which is tainted by our experiences, is why we seek out self-healing at all.

Children thrive more on the non-verbal communication of their caregivers than they do the actual words. Programming may be more overt, like the crushing feeling of a degrading comment. You want to be a lawyer? A parent may reply, "I don't think you have the grades to accomplish that." An aspiring professional football player's father may scoff and say, "That is *not* in your future." But what creates the shame? The scar is the non-verbal detachment of the parent, the neglect, the lack of eye contact, the lack of hugging or worse, the physical abuse. The broken glass in your lenses may be fragments from all sorts of scenarios. You will likely discover these fragments as you untangle your view and you begin to notice that your glasses are not *fitting* you any longer.

Our parents are living through their own tainted filters, which were passed down to them through programming by *their* struggling and conflicted parents. These patterns are ancestral. Children take on these tainted filters of our own parents when we are children, and then spend our adult lives tearing them apart with the goal of finally finding ourselves. Do children honestly have a shot at following their own soul's path, allowing The Universe to hear their desires and help to manifest their dreams?

Some do. I didn't.

I see now how I view and experience the world through the emotional scars that I formed in childhood. Every painful moment stored in my body is waiting for a future moment to rear its ugly head. My mother's abuse and neglect formed me into a young woman who kept up a firm wall of energetic protection; an "I don't need anyone" persona. This worked well for me until it didn't, and it stopped working when the buried emotions began seeping through every pore and cell of my body. I just couldn't hold them in any longer.

It was time for me to get new glasses.

Whether programming is overt or subliminal, children listen and make adjustments in order to be loved and accepted by their parents. This is also the reason children of abusive parents don't speak up against our abuser: because we love them on some level and don't want them to be angry with us for speaking the truth that lurks beneath the surface. We learn to hide ourselves first out of survival, and then as a habit. Both as children and adults, the desired outcome of hiding ourselves is clear: we want to be loved and accepted. I understood through the behavior of my mother that I was not loved. Both her words and her non-verbal behavior left my brain stuck in survival mode. And, as only a child could, I tried to make sense of why she was always mad at or ignoring me. The child brain cannot understand anything other than "I am bad, and who I am needs to change fundamentally in order to be loved."

As a child, I did not possess the wisdom to understand why my mother acted in the manner she did. When she would ignore me, I learned to be quiet, small, and "good," hoping that this change would turn me into someone different—someone better that she would love. It worked, and my mother tormented me less when I didn't come out of my bedroom or when I was very, very quiet in the house. I became small and isolated myself, trying to adapt to my environment and make it safe.

However, the true me was never small, quiet, and timid. The real me was (and is) flamboyant, boisterous, strong-willed, and happy. I was hiding the real me because she didn't respond well to happy, playful, boisterous Ashley. My mother was mean to me when I acted how I felt on the inside. It was instinct, so I started behaving the opposite because I was trying to be loved.

Children need to be loved; it is how we survive and thrive. There have been many studies done with infants in orphanages on what a physical and emotional connection does to the development of infants. If a child is left alone, isolated, and not talked to or touched, their brain will literally go into shutdown mode; they will become sickly and unwell. On the other hand, if a child is shown attention, if they can feel love from a caregiver's eyes, they will develop on a normal trajectory. In the middle, if the child cannot count on the affection or if the affection is conditional, the child will try to adapt themselves to their environment in order to survive.

As adults, children of abusive parents will hide themselves from co-workers, friends, and lovers at all costs in order to feel loved and accepted. This façade is driven by a fear of being unlovable and unworthy—a fear that likely was true at some point in their life. There is a time for all abused children when we begin to believe and accept the adaptive persona as the real self. We literally abandon ourselves in survival.

Then, as we forge through the pathways of healing, we begin searching and seeking out the reasons behind why we are not happy, feeling fulfilled, or connected to our life purpose, and we discover that we have been hiding ourselves from the world. Healing from trauma will lead us through self-discovery. There, we uncover our authentic self, understand and identify our scars, repair our glasses, leave behind the adaptive persona and learn to love ourselves as we are. Uncovering our authentic self means that we must go within and connect to this part of us, the part we have been ignoring in order to feel loved. Ninety percent of the time, the parts of us that we ignore and push down are indeed our authentic parts. (I'll talk more about how to do this in later chapters.)

Before we can uncover the real us, we must first observe the places in our lives in which we have scars, the place where we first adapted our survival persona. Once we identify our adaptive persona and begin to unpack the feelings of the child inside of us who simply wants to be loved, we discover that loving ourselves is the first step in creating meaningful, safe, and loving relationships. We cannot truly know or love ourselves until we have broken through the walls of our adaptive persona. Therefore, we must ask, "Who am I trying to be, and why?"

When we are stuck living through our façade, we become unhappy with our relationships, unhappy with our work, the list goes on… and this is all because we are hiding who we really are. Simply stated, if we say to the world that we like blueberry muffins when we don't, and thus we are given a blueberry muffin at the office each day by a friendly co-worker, we are starting off our workday with something that displeases us. It is not the muffin that bothers us, it is the fact that we said we liked them in the first place when we knew we didn't. It is living unauthentically that creates the feelings of discomfort. Again, we must ask, "If I do not like blueberry muffins, why have I said I do? Who was I seeking approval from in this situation? Why did I not feel as if I could say that indeed I do not like blueberry muffins?"

Whether it is blueberry muffins, a sexually harassing co-worker, a cheating boyfriend, or an abusive parent, it is our inherent right to claim ownership for our *yes* and our *no*. It is our responsibility to connect to our inner voice, our soul, and then to speak our truth.

What are you *not* saying?

The words I often used when trying to describe the emotions I felt due my mother's lack of authenticity were confusion and disbelief, likely because those are the emotions I often felt when I caught her lying. My mother manipulated her friends and family, telling them she was the victim of a terribly mean daughter.

One summer at the beach, a friend of my mother's pulled me aside and gave me a talking to. "Listen, you need to be a little nicer to your mother," she said. "Stop giving her such a hard time. She is upset all the time because of how you treat her. She works hard and she is a good mother, she doesn't deserve you to treat her like this."

Why would she say I was the bad one and my mother was the good one? It didn't make sense. Just the evening before, my mother sat in silence at our dinner table. She didn't speak a single word to me. As I tried to eat dinner, picking at my food, my stomach revolted. My gut churned with worry that I had done something wrong; something I couldn't identify no matter how hard I tried.

On the evenings she would ignore me, I often sat in the silence wondering what was going to happen next. I was waiting for the next shoe to drop. The conflict and the confusion I felt was stewing inside every cell of my body, and I was trapped in my mother's black hole of inauthenticity. She would abuse, neglect, and ignore me for days and made *me* out to be the abuser. She was pretending that she loved me and that I was hurting her, but she was lying... and I was trapped.

I was caught in the conflict of her lies, and the struggle to be authentic was slowly taking form in my brain and body. I was hiding my truth, and all my body knew was that I was not living an authentic life. That was something my mother and I shared. I was feeling hurt, confused, and angry at my mother for her outlandish lying, and yet I never told the truth to the people who believed her lies. As the child, I didn't actually have a voice. Most abused children don't.

My reason for being inauthentic was out of survival, not because I was lying manipulatively. But reasoning the why didn't matter to my brain, and it formed a habit regardless of whether it came out of a need to survive or not. This quickly turned into hiding the truth. I was convinced people would not have believed me if I told them what was really happening. They believed her lies. The second habitual belief that came out of a childhood full of conflicted emotions and disbelief was that people who lived inauthentically were not safe people for me to be around.

I experienced a lot of anxiety around people who were not living an authentic life, and for years, I wasn't able to understand why. Oftentimes it was around women who appeared to be happy and have it all that I felt the most panicked. I associated what I understood as their materialism to be a quality I never wanted to have in my own life.

As I was trying to figure out who and what I wanted to become, I was closely watching everyone around me. Over the years, I was introduced to many women who looked and felt the same to me. They were wealthy, married to powerful men, and dripping in designer clothes and perfectly styled hair. Most didn't work; they lunched.

This is not a stereotype—these are real women who, over the course of 15 years, I have met at business dinners and various other parts of my life. Some were married to my husband's colleagues, and others I met out and about. They were miserable but worked hard to hide it. Some of them would tell me they hated their husbands, wished they were allowed to work, wanted to get divorced but were afraid to, or simply complained about their life. I wondered if I was the only one they were telling these secrets to, because to everyone else around us, they appeared to live the perfect life. I didn't like knowing how they really felt while watching them fake it around other people. It made me anxious because they were lying. They were not only lying to the people around them, but they were lying to themselves. And because lies hurt people, lies scare me.

I was terrified of the conflicted lives they were living, but I was uneducated on why I felt this way. I didn't have the tools to examine my feelings, so I labeled their materialism as bad. I vowed to never become a rich housewife who stayed in her unhappy marriage for the money. However, the one and only thing this label did for me was rob me of the ability to enjoy the hard work of my husband and the wonderful material things we were accumulating. I was so caught up in running away from the feelings of what having nice things meant—thinking that I was a bad person—that I never enjoyed what we had.

The most important takeaway from this period of my life was that it was not their expensive pocketbooks, lunch calendar, or designer clothes that I was afraid of. What I was afraid of was their lack of authenticity; how they were feeling on the inside was not what they were showing on the outside.

That, my friends, is a hard-wired trauma trigger for me. My mother lied to everyone about what our life was like behind closed doors. I was always unsafe because of her lies. I was scared for these women, and I was feeling their pain like it was mine. My nervous system would go into overdrive when I was around them because it thought I was the one who was unsafe and trapped in a life of lies. My brain thought I was the one who was lying.

There were people in my inner circle and family who also lived inauthentic lives. I saw these people often, and the triggers were constant and hard for me to escape. For example, a close relative of mine suffered in addiction while her entire family acquiesced to her behavior for years, unwilling to admit they had an addict in the family. Her family chose to ignore her addiction because it would have made them imperfect, and being a perfect family was something they had pride in.

Learning to live authentically in the face of those who are not requires boundaries—a vital relationship tool that abused children often have no idea how to utilize. Boundaries are uncomfortable for everyone when first established, and there will always be someone who refuses to accept them. Usually, we need boundaries the most with the person who is most vocal about the boundaries. This is usually the same person who hurts us the most as well.

What abused children do is rationalize the behavior of those who hurt us. We excuse them and usually find fault within our own behaviors to take responsibility for the poor treatment. But psychoanalyzing the people who hurt us doesn't make how they treat us not hurt. The wisdom that comes from analyzing other's behaviors leaves us with guilt and shame for wanting them to change, rather than giving us what we need in the relationship. It is perfectly OK for people to live the way they want to live, but when their behavior is affecting us in a negative way, we need boundaries in order for our nervous systems to feel safe again.

When I first began establishing healthy boundaries instead of black and white ones, I felt stuck in an inauthentic life. It felt wrong for me to be mean to people who hurt me, and because I was not grounded in boundaries, I never told them I was hurt—which ended me in circumstances where I had to fake being nice to someone who I was truly angry with. Before I began the work, if a friend upset me or we had a falling out, I would cut them off. I used my simple math formula and assumed that if they hurt me, that meant they didn't love me and thus couldn't be trusted. This wasn't so easy to do with family.

As I healed, I learned to have more compassion for both myself *and* others. I came to understand that it was possible to keep people in my life even though our relationship was changing, and even if they hurt me on some level. Setting healthy boundaries such as choosing when and which family functions I attended, what I was willing to keep discussing, and how long I stayed helped me to feel safe. I listened to my inner child, as she was the one who guided me on the boundaries I needed to establish with my family.

Some relationships simply fade away; it's just a part of life. However, I found it difficult to manage seeing the people I was letting fade away. Being nice to them when we crossed paths made me feel like I was pretending to be their friend. Never haven spoken up about how I truly felt in the relationship and letting it fizzle out was one thing, but having to see and mingle with them was a complete trigger for me. It felt fake; like I was lying.

I would have chosen to never see these old friends again, but we share mutual friends, so that just wasn't a possibility. What I needed to do was establish boundaries. I began by asking myself what I needed in the relationship to feel safe. Most of what I needed, I knew I was not going to get directly from them, so I created my own safety features that I built into the occasions when I knew I was going to see them:

1. I limited my time in the groups when we crossed paths. If I had to go to a party where these friends were, I would stay for a short while then leave, always keeping a close watch on how I was feeling. If my anxiety was increasing, I would leave sooner than planned.

2. If I got caught in a situation where we ended up alone talking, I would excuse myself and go to the bathroom. Once I was in the bathroom, I could take deep breaths and tell myself that I was safe. I reminded myself over and over that being nice didn't mean that was ignoring my feelings of hurt.

3. I had a bag of tricks in my pocket at all times. These were tools that I used to calm myself down. I had a piece of paper that had three sentences written on it: "You are safe" "Stressful events don't have to bring on physical pain" and "Don't feel guilty for having boundaries." I kept lavender essential oil to breath in, calming my nervous system, and cards for playing solitaire in case I needed a break from the crowd. I could play in a quiet corner, if the scenario allowed. I also always kept earbuds in my purse. In an event where my anxiety was taking over, I would pop them in and listen to Liquid Mind on Pandora while pretending I was going to the bathroom.

These tricks got me out of some stressful situations as I established boundaries with people who hurt me. The main purpose of my bag of tricks was to calm my nervous system down so that it could ascertain it was in the present moment (and not in my childhood home). It allowed in wisdom to see that these old friends were also on their own healing journeys, and it was likely that how they treated me didn't have much to do with me, but way more to do with their own stuff.

As time went on, and as I had more interactions with them, my brain and body got on the same page. I knew that I was safe no matter what. I was able to experience feelings that were conflicted, acknowledge that I had these hurt feelings, and was then able to be cordial to those who hurt me. I was loosening my grip on black and white thinking. Once my nervous system was on the mend, I found it easier to apply the wisdom of my healing to the analysis of their behavior. They had their own trauma-colored lenses with which they viewed life. Together, calming my system and telling my brain it was safe, while applying the wisdom and knowledge of who these people were, brought me to a new understanding of who I am. This was a sure sign I was healing.

Learning these triggers was so freeing for me. I don't hide my nice jewelry anymore, and I enjoy driving expensive cars without guilt. What made the women I observed inauthentic was that they were miserable, yet wanting the world to think otherwise. I am not miserable behind closed doors, and I am not them. I was applying the black and white thinking of their façade to my life. I jumped to label nice clothes and expensive things as bad. The items themselves are not inherently bad, but when you use them as a way to hide from the world, they become ugly.

For me, being authentic means speaking my truth—the truth of how I feel, even if I only speak this truth to myself. Allowing my feelings to present themselves, noticing them, acknowledging them, and then realizing that I am safe while I experience emotions is how I live each day. What this means is I show up, keep it real, and feel my feelings. If the situation calls for me to be around those who have hurt me, I can still be nice and feel sad at the same time.

I went through a whole process to learn how to hold inside and live with two big emotions at once. That process takes as long as it takes; you can't rush it. I am grateful that I was able to go through this and unlearn unhealthy patterns of behavior. It is important for me to feel and express my emotions as they are; to live the same life outside as the one that happens behind closed doors. Not everyone can do this, some are just trying to survive.

We all have our own reasons for when we are inauthentic, our own set of circumstances that molded us, and how that process unfolds uniquely. When we experience what we feel, we are authentic. When we hide ourselves, we lie. When we choose to refrain from self-expression while fully aware of the process and why, we apply discrimination.

So, I'll ask you again: what are you not *saying?*

Spend some time taking inventory in your own life and ask the following questions:

Is there somewhere in your life you aren't showing up as your true self? Perhaps it's with a specific person or at work.

Once you've identified those areas or people, how does that make you feel?

Part 4

The Work

Chapter 27
Majestic Woman

The first time I met my authentic self was the most shocking and magical moment I have ever had. It was during my very first acupuncture appointment in 2008. Nicholas was almost three, and I was starting to take care of myself again. I was getting further away from living in fight or flight each day, and I was trying acupuncture to relieve some lower back pain that I was having.

It makes me laugh now when I think about it—I had *no* idea that chronic lower back pain is an indication of trauma and trapped emotions of feeling unsafe. I was unaware at this point that my physical ailments were an indication of my trapped emotions. I was simply going to acupuncture to relieve back pain as so many of my friends were doing. The Eastern vibe in the clinic was calming and comforting. As I lay on the table, I felt hopeful that I was finally going to get some pain relief.

I instantly loved my therapist and owner of the clinic, Lisa Spellmen. She placed the needles in my arms, legs, abdomen, and face, and then told me to take a nap as she left me alone in the room. As soon as I closed my eyes, I felt my body become heavy. Beyond the darkness of my closed eyes, I started seeing colors flying around in my head, swirls all running into one another. Although my eyes were closed, the colors and their energy engulfed my whole body, and I felt them all around me as if they, too, were in the room with me.

Far off into the distance of my vision, I saw a woman sitting by the edge of a cliff overlooking the ocean. She had her knees pulled up to her chest, and the wind was blowing her long hair. She was in a faint black shadow mist, and I couldn't see her skin tone or the color of her hair. She didn't have a face, either. Still, I was drawn to her and the energy that she was giving off. The air around her was calm and centered, and she appeared to be happy and content.

I walked up to her, but she didn't turn to look at me. As I sat down next to her, it was as if I could see what she was seeing, and when I looked out onto the water, all the colors were now in front of my eyes out before us. The water was electric blue, and the air even had a wispy white color and texture. Sitting next to this majestic woman, my mind ran through many thoughts all at once, but not one of them made any sense to me. It was like I was getting a download of information, but it was in a code I didn't know how to crack. Yet, at the same time, it all made sense to me; the massive amount of information and visions I was seeing. They felt familiar, as if I had heard and seen them before.

When the doorknob in the acupuncture room clicked, my dream-like state came to a crashing halt. My acupuncture session was over, and I was never the same again. I was in a loopy, relaxed state, and I drove home the completely wrong way.

I wasn't aware of thinking again about my majestic woman, nor did I have another experience quite like it. Years later, she came back to me and I finally recognized her as my soul. Perhaps that is why she didn't have skin tone or appear to me as a human that first time.

As I unconsciously continued my quest to find the feelings I experienced at that first time together, I began using deep guided meditations. It was during one of these that we met again three years later. I didn't set out with the intention of finding her during this meditation, it just happened. I was listening to a guided meditation that brought me deep into an almost-sleeplike state. The voice brought me through a field into the forest, and with every guided turn I fell deeper into relaxation. I was simply following my prompts, allowing myself to slow my breathing and let my body feel heavy.

At the point in the meditation where the voice asked me to just rest, it happened. Again, she sat waiting for me on the edge of her cliff overlooking the ocean. Only this time when I sat down next to her, I became her. We were one. My body began to vibrate, and we lay down on her cliff. Without understanding it, I knew that we became one so her energy could heal my body. I let it happen, and then the voice prompted me to come back through the woods back into the present moment.

As quickly as it happened, it ended; and I was changed forever again.

Around this time, my father had given me Brian Weiss's book *Many Lives Many Masters*. He thought it may help me as I healed from our time in the hospital with Nicholas. The words on the pages came alive for me. Brian was explaining the idea of our soul as a concept I had come to not only understand intellectually but also felt for myself through Reiki sessions with Lucinda and in my own meditations. I finished the book in two days, and when I closed the cover, I said to myself, "I was never alone. My soul has been with me all along. That is why when I met her on the mountaintop she felt so familiar to me. That is why we became one the second time we met; it was my earthly body and my ego that had us feeling separate, but we have always been one."

In meditation, people often set an intention before they begin their practice. As an example, you could set an intention to open your heart to be more loving, use your voice more, or even to meet your soul. Whatever it is, intentions must be considered seeds. You can't force anything to happen in meditation. We can set the intent but then must wait for it to happen as it may. There is also a difference between setting an intention to meet your soul during a mediation, and simply meditating and going into the gap in between your thoughts and getting lost there. And maybe, just maybe, when you are lost in the gap, you will have a majestic experience with your soul. I typically don't set intentions before I meditate. I focus on a Sanskrit mantra that has no English meaning. Doing this allows my brain to physically not have a focus, and when your mind allows you to stay in the gap between your thoughts, your soul takes over and you are no longer living in the conscious realm.

I have guided many people through their meditation practices, and I tell all my students the same thing: What happens during my meditation can't happen for you in the same way because we are different people having different experiences. What I *can* tell you is that when you meditate and you slip into the gap between your thoughts, you are indeed connecting to your soul. But other than that, it differs for everyone.

It may not be a magical or majestic experience, or it may be. You could have one off the charts meditation and then never again have anything like that happen.

As I did, you will know for certain any meaningful and profound meeting you may have with yourself is real, because nothing else will make sense. It is a feeling that is all-knowing. That is how I knew, once I opened my eyes at the end of my meditation, that I had again met my soul. I knew because I could not have planned a more beautiful creature, I could not have conjured up in my mind anything like what I saw or felt. There are no human words to describe this when it happens. I was blown away on every level. I felt full and alive.

Only this feeling didn't last for too long.

Once I had entered into and seen the infinitude of my soul, I constantly tried to get back to that feeling. Who wouldn't want to feel that freedom, that peace and harmony again and again. I read books on living a spiritual life, I took classes on the law of attraction, I studied and studied to no avail. I was trying to force the peace, comfort, and happiness I felt in acupuncture and again during my meditation. I was desperate to have the same feelings every day. Is that even possible for the most enlightened ones, to always be on the beam? I didn't know, but I was trying.

A teacher of mine, Lisa Campion, author of *Psychic Reiki and Energy Healing for Empaths*, gave me the book *After Ecstasy, then Laundry* by Jack Kornfield. I read the book in just a few days, and it was a game changer for me. I had a one-on-one session with her one evening after her Psychic Reiki class, and asked her, "So wait, you can be a regular person and be enlightened at the same time?"

Lisa laughed with me and said, "Yes!" I was trying to find a feeling that may very well never happen again for me and talking that through with Lisa helped me to grasp those fleeting moments for what they are—fleeting. Powerful, but fleeting. We were not meant to stay in that enlightened state as humans all day long, otherwise we would forget to do the laundry!

I was trying to learn something new, forgetting that my mind, body, and soul already knew this feeling of utter peace. What I needed to do was remember that my soul was always there, I didn't need a class to bring me back home. I needed to slow down and go within. I used to spend hours taking classes on how to connect with my spirit guides or how to find inner peace; all searching for something that was already within me.

The next day, after my session with Lisa, I returned to the grind of work: speeches and TV interviews about One Mission. I thought that living this life of duality, businesswoman and spiritual woman was contradictory. I thought it had to be all one way or it meant I was faking half of my life.

Black and white thinking, my friends! Of course I thought that way, that I couldn't be a badass businesswoman and a spiritual leader in the same life...

The balance of living a spiritual life, soul living and living in a human body with an ego and past trauma, is a push and pull that goes on and on like the waves of the ocean.

At this stage of my healing, I began to get angry and frustrated with myself and those around me. I had met my soul, and I now had the knowledge of how it felt to be alive with divine energy and the pure light from The Universe. Yet I was still having low voltage feelings like jealousy, anger, and fear, which was frustrating because I knew deep inside that was not my true self. When I was with my majestic woman, everything made sense, I felt no anger and I was at peace; when I was not sitting in easy pose meditating, I was living a human life and those are hard.

This is where my healing stayed for many years: frustrated with human life and not knowing what the heck I was doing on the spiritual side. The frustration I felt with trying to live my authentic life was a starting point for me to begin looking inward and asking myself deep, soul-level questions such as, "Who am I? What do I truly want? What is my life's purpose?"

I sat in this chaos for years, roughly five years before I crashed and burned with migraines. I was constantly searching, always looking outward for answers in books, classes, and healers. I was struggling with emotions that were deep inside me trying to come out, and I had no idea how to even feel them. I was confused on how to lead a happy healthy life because to me, it wasn't a straightforward answer; it wasn't just about making the decision to be happy. I would have made changes if I knew how or what to change. I was lost, and I needed a guide.

I knew I wanted to be free. I wanted to have the capacity to be fully me, but I had no idea who that was.

There were moments when I liked being referred to as the power couple, as Ari and I were seen by many people. I did thrive off people telling me how amazing I was, and how they wished they could be as inspiring. However, compliments like that felt good for a minute, and then I felt empty again. I mean, their words were true: what I was doing for my community was meaningful, and I did inspire others to become their best self. But none of that matters when you go to bed feeling like you aren't good enough. In the long run, compliments actually made me feel worse.

When you are not living an authentic life, you see compliments as lies because you think the people giving them don't really know you. I would force a smile and say, "Thank you so much, I am so honored that you feel that way," but what the smile really meant was, "I am happy to hear your praise; but I don't think you really know me; if you did, you would never say that."

The only times I felt free was when I was meditating, but we can't use meditation as a way to escape our life—that isn't the point! So, I hid my spiritual, healing side from the business side of my life. I never got the memo that I could just be me in every aspect of my life. That stems from my mother never accepting me as I was and lying to everyone about our life together. It was another hard-wired thinking pattern that I applied to my adult life: *Don't be the real you and hide what is really going on.*

Not only did I not understand that I could stand tall in my complex nature and it would be OK, but I was so worried about being authentic that I never saw my own truth. I was hiding, bouncing in between the life I was living and the spiritual life I was searching for. I was still so fragmented in my pain that there was no way I could have understood that I was both. I wasn't bouncing in between two worlds; I was the CEO of a successful non-profit and I was a healer on her own path of healing. All of it was true. All of it was me.

It was almost 10 years before I was able to put the pieces of myself back together. I was living this all the while, just not as the me I am today.

The soul-level questions are still a part of my daily meditation practice. As I pose them at the beginning of my morning and afternoon meditations sessions, I am asking to connect to my soul. The answers come in time.

They unfold and present to me when everything is ready to blossom into manifestation.

At times, we all get caught up in not living authentically. This is not an indication of failure or one not being spiritual, rather it is an opportunity for change.

If you are feeling this calling, just take the first step and let the rest unfold. You know you have fallen off the path of authenticity when you are feeling uncomfortable, anxious, or are in pain.

Be open to observing yourself in these times and go inward, asking yourself: Who am I? What do I want? Do I have any unmet needs that are pushing hidden emotions to the surface? Journal it out, let your soul speak to you.

I know firsthand how scary and alone it can feel to simply *be* you, the person that only you know. Hear me when I say this: You can both be scared and be courageous. I promise you that the feelings of fear about being you will diminish far faster than the feelings of unhappiness as you try to be someone you are not.

Chapter 28
The Work

I was unaware while it was happening, but I was healing all along my journey of pain and suffering. Once I officially began to heal, I could see how the pit stops I had made along the way were laying the foundation for the heavy lifting I was going to do with my therapist, Anna.

My first, and likely my most important pit stop, was finding Deepak Chopra's meditation CDs and starting a meditation practice (which made it so sweet that later on I would become a Chopra certified meditation teacher). Later, when I began receiving Reiki with Lucinda, I was giving my body strength and healing directly from The Universe. These sessions were providing me strength as a physical foundation for healing. It is difficult to heal spiritually if our bodies are not strong enough to funnel the energy of healing. The opposite is also true—that when we need to heal spiritually, our physical bodies will become ill if we have let it go unattended too long. Then, with each acupuncture session, and every book I read or class I took on how to manage my energy, I was giving my body the power it needed to get stronger and heal.

When we heal, we must first strip, and the stripping hurts and takes time. There is no way that my body or spirit would have been able to heal if I had started to rip off scabs and wounds like a band-aid. My foundation would not have held me up. Believe it or not, our pain and story do serve a purpose for a while, even as we are shedding it.

When I decided I was ready to heal back in 2010, if I would have been stripped of every bad thing that ever happened to me, I would have been standing before this world completely naked and without support. Even the story we hold onto provides support. But we must heal slowly and methodically in order to protect the foundation, and in order to protect the foundation, we must strengthen it first. That is what I was doing with every healer I went to, and every kundalini yoga class I took, and every meditation I squeezed in. I was strengthening my foundation so that I could eventually gut the house without it all collapsing.

Patience is a crucial player in the arena of healing. We cannot rush this process. People told me that all the time, but I wanted to be the exception to that rule. I was so uncomfortable that I would have done anything to get through as many stages of healing as quickly as I could. I wanted the fast-track lane; the VIP experience. The hilarious part of this whole thing is that I actually thought I was fast-tracking at one point. I can remember thinking, *OK great, glad that is done! Now I can get on with my life.* Unfortunately, this was right before I fell apart. I had gone through a rough patch of mother issues during a psychic development class I was taking with Lisa Campion.

I was having trouble discerning the messages I was receiving during my client sessions, unclear if they were for me or for my clients. I was getting mad at myself for not being able to grasp this concept as quickly as I thought my peers were. I went to my teacher Lisa for help, and she explained to me that I needed to let go of some past trauma that was holding me back from being able to get clear messages.

In a session with her, my feelings of not being good enough came up in full force. It was as if I was living my childhood all over again, and my mother was telling me that I looked fat in an outfit or punishing me for not picking up my room. I was the little girl who felt small and stupid. Lisa placed her hands on my heart and I began to sob. I told her that it was my mother; that I felt like I wasn't going to be a good healer because my mother told me that I wasn't ever good enough. This was a big epiphany for me in my healing. Up to that point, I had not made the connection between my own feelings of inadequacy at my job and feelings of anxiety due to how I was raised.

I felt like I had hit the jackpot. Halleluiah, I was healed! Things were going to be better now.

If only healing was a one and done! The truth is, it just isn't. What I needed to do was take that epiphany and learn from it. I needed to ask myself where in my life I was feeling inadequate or not worthy, and what relationships triggered this inside me. I needed to dissect all the places in my life where the wound of not being loved unconditionally was showing up, and then heal from there. Instead, I would leave my sessions with Lisa thinking I had solved all my problems, and then I would be shocked when the same topic would rear its ugly head again. But the work is multi-dimensional; we can't just observe and release, we also need to give ourselves a voice and make connections before we can truly heal.

I wouldn't change any part of my journey now that I am through the thick of it. Truly, I would not change a single thing, even being sick in bed for almost five months. I would not be where I am today without having had gone through each moment of pain (and each subsequent moment of healing). I went through many stages of healing, and I am sure you will also. The work changed for me as I was ready to heal at new and different stages, and I had to gain resources and strength for each of them.

I knew I was on the right track when my migraines began to lessen and go away. That was a clear indication that the work was indeed working. However, once I got through that pink phase of initial emotional release and pain relief, life began to happen again, and I'd often get triggered and headaches would hit me. They were not as bad or as frequent, but when stressful events occurred or I was not listening to a child part of me, I'd have symptoms. Here is where the step of observation came in.

Prior to beginning the work with Anna, I didn't have any idea I was being triggered until it was too late. These moments are referred to as "off the beam"—you are no longer in tune with the work you have been doing. It's like you forgot everything you learned. The easiest place for me to observe when I am off the beam is in my marriage. Marriage is where people experience most of their triggers, and I am no exception.

The years I spent disconnected from my emotions were the years Ari and I fought the most intensely. I am Italian and he is Greek, so these fights were usually epic, and they lasted for days. Almost every argument we had stemmed from a ridiculous comment said by one of us, usually in jest.

One summer evening in 2011, Ari and I were in the kitchen talking about business. I was telling him about my new plan to raise money for One Mission and working out some numbers with him. I had them all wrong, and he just laughed at me. "You are being stupid," he laughed, "that isn't how you do that math."

He called me stupid, and that is all I heard. Not that I was *being* stupid, which was still not nice to say; but I heard him call me stupid. I was so upset I got in my car and left. The devastation I felt when we would argue like that was immense because he was the only person, other than my father, that I ever trusted. I let my guard down with Ari like I have never done with any other man, and I felt abandoned and abused when we would fight. How could the love of my life refer to me as stupid?

Once we finally talked and Ari apologized, he explained to me that clearly, he doesn't think I am stupid, he just poorly chose words in saying my math was funky. I calmed down in the moment, but those feelings of devastation and abandonment were piling up. And they didn't originate from the arguments with Ari—they were from my mother and my past. It was my relationship with my husband that was providing me a mirror to show me all the places I was off the beam, for which I am eternally grateful. We came to earth together to create big things, my husband and me. We came here together to create powerful children, build businesses that change the lives of those who work in them, and most importantly, to invoke change within each other. Ari and I are cosmically connected. This is not our first lifetime together, and it will not be our last.

I didn't understand then that I was trying so hard to show everyone in my life that I was smart, caring, and a good person because I thought that would make them love me. Remember that children need to feel loved in order to feel safe. These trigger moments were getting to old wounds of my childhood; specifically, the wound that I am not loveable. Often, it is as if we are unconscious before we begin healing. I was unaware that I was being triggered, and I was clearly unaware of why I felt the emotional spark in the first place. We are usually never upset with the current situation; we are feeling emotions of our pasts.

My body didn't know the difference between being told I was stupid by my mother, how that made me feel unsafe, and how it was triggered when my husband laughed at my math. My nervous system thought I was 8 years old again, back in my childhood home. This is what the work is for, rewiring the brain and nervous system so that it can see present situations for the present and not the past. This took months upon months of chipping away at all of the trapped emotions and allowing them to come up, then making the connections to the moment my nervous system first got hit with the trauma, and then training my brain to see the present situation as new.

I believe having a meditation practice is a must for anyone wishing to make change in their life. What I often hear from my clients and friends is that they know they should meditate, but they just can't find the time. I heard Peter Crone, The Mind Architect, say once that we need to stop "shoulding" on ourselves! This is so true. You only need to begin a practice if you are feeling called to do so. If you feel the calling and have a desire, then and only then you can begin "shoulding" on yourself. Once you have made the decision to begin a practice, you can say things like "I *should* find time to meditate today," or "I *shouldn't* skip my afternoon meditation session."

You see, meditating is just like going to the gym. When you begin an exercise regimen, you don't show up on day one and hit it hard like a pro, and then wake up the next day looking buff and feeling strong. In fact, the opposite actually happens. You start off slow, feel sore, and usually give up, stop going to the gym all together, and then a few weeks later you get back on the horse. Building a strong body is very similar to building a strong mind and connection to your spirit. You have to take the first step, then, you must stay dedicated and eventually it will all pay off. Additionally, the busier you are, the more you need to meditate; you can't use that as an excuse. Busy people need more downtime. It gives them clarity on projects and calms the nervous system so it can get ready for battle the next day. Meditation keeps busy people heathy enough to keep their pace for the long haul.

The biggest misconception about meditation is that the goal is to empty your mind. That is not the case. Nobody is able to completely turn off their brain—unless they are either in a coma or dead! So, let's take that off the table, OK? You are always going to have thoughts, even when you have been meditating for years and years. Your brain is designed to think, and think it will.

Once you find the form of meditation that fits you best and you are deep into your practice, you will find your mind wanders. Mine does, too. All you are to do when this happens is to gently and simply come back to your practice; come back to your mantra or your breath. Keep your focus there, and when the mind wanders again as it will, gently come back. You will do this over and over throughout your sessions. Focus, wander, focus, wander.

It may even look like this, too: Focus, wander, focus, wander, focus, get mad at yourself (this is still a wander), focus, totally lose focus for what seems like forever, get mad at yourself for not being able to focus, focus, wander, focus, think to yourself I must have ADD why can't I stay focused… wait how much time has gone by? I am terrible at meditating.

Now, over time, your wandering will decrease. The space in between the distractions is called the "gap," and it is within the gap that you are able to connect deeply to your soul. This is when you are your most rested in meditation and your brain waves may look like you are sleeping even while you are awake. My resting heart rate while I meditate can go into the low 40s. You may experience peaks of distractibility as you meditate during stressful periods of your life, when you have a lot of things going on. All of this is normal, so just go with it. Remember, it isn't about getting to any destination during meditation, it is about the practice.

Meditation gives your mind and body a literal break from life. It is a time of restoration. For many, it can also be a time for manifesting and creating because when you shut out the outside world, you're better able to connect to the soul within. Remember that it is our soul that is driving the bus here, so connecting to it is how we find guidance during difficult times, or find new opportunities in life. When we are distracted with running, working, TV, social media and so on, we are not giving ourselves the opportunity to listen to what is within all of us: the deep desires of our soul.

I have been working with people for years using Reiki, meditation, and journaling, and I have found that meditation will have the most profound impact if you simply give it a try. You can begin using apps if that feels easier—my favorite is Headspace. Whatever it is you try, what I do recommend is starting off slowly. Don't try to do a 45-minute chakra clearing and soul connection guided meditation with someone who is selling their method on Instagram.

Meditation is as old as dirt, and while some people have some really cool methods out there to try, I recommend keeping it simple to start. Deepak Chopra has some amazing mantra meditations. I am a certified Chopra Center teacher and I teach my students Primordial Sound mantra-based meditation. I also used Headspace for about a year and I loved it. In Headspace, the focus is about breath work. You will need to find the method that works best for you, so I recommend trying each to see which one feels right to you. Start off with 10 minutes twice a day, and work your way up from there.

Again, try to remember that it isn't about achieving any goal in meditation—it is about the journey. You will have ups and downs; there will be times you feel amazing and are convinced that the work is truly benefitting you, and other times you may feel down in the dumps and totally off track. Meditation is profound, and will also likely stir up some dust within you. I always think it is a good idea to have a coach or a buddy of sorts when you begin so that you can talk about what changes your body is going through. Try to roll with whatever comes during your practice. There is no perfect person, no perfect meditation practice, and certainly no perfect life.

Chapter 29
Nose Ring

*I*n the middle of writing this book, I got a burning desire to get my nose pierced. I downloaded an app that allows you to add things to your photo, like a nose piercing. I opened the picture and showed my kids.

"So what do you think?" I asked.

My daughters freaked out. Zoe started crying, and Eleni practically screamed, "Absolutely not! Mom, stop! You are NOT 26!" Their reaction surprised me—they know I have five tattoos and were excited when I got my last one just a few months before this conversation.

I stood before them wanting so badly to confess all I was feeling; to say this is who I really am, and that for all their years I have been struggling to break free and show up as me. I have always wanted more tattoos, and I wish I kept my tongue ring and my eyebrow piercing. But I took them out to conform to the world a long time ago.

Back in 1997, I was working for Fidelity, answering incoming phone calls for the 403b retirement plans. That year, I went on spring break and got my tongue and eyebrow pierced. I rationalized these piercings in terms of my job by saying it was OK because I never actually saw clients in person.

The calls were usually from clients asking to take money out of their retirement accounts. I sourced and poorly handled hundreds of calls before I politely got asked to leave because my customer service skills were lacking in a big way. Call after call, the clients yelled at me, "You can't tell me that my money isn't mine to take out when I please!" Of course, the callers had no idea that it was not Fidelity that made the rules; it was their HR department. I must have recited the same thing hundreds of times: "Ma'am, I suggest that you call your HR department to discuss your concerns. I am only able to move money from allocation to allocation and I am not authorized to make any withdrawals."

It was the day I got into a yelling match with a customer that my boss called me into his office and played back the tape for me. I cringed as I listened to my scoffing and interrupting the client, finally telling her she was acting like an ass and wasting my time.

"Ashley, working behind a desk isn't a good fit for you. Customer service isn't a good fit for you. You need to work somewhere that gives you more creative freedom," he said. As he talked, I was trying to hide my tongue ring from him, but I found myself playing with it as the word freedom rolled off his tongue. *Yes, freedom! That is my ticket. I want to be free to be me!*

It was my father who ultimately convinced me to take it out. "Sorry, Peach," he said, "but people just won't take you seriously if you have a tongue ring." My father was right—the world makes judgments based on appearances.

I hid the piercing from my boss for weeks, and then I made the decision to take it out. My conflict is I actually think I did the right thing back then, taking the piercings out. However, it was still my choice to conform. *My choice.*

I believe there is a place for everyone in this world, we simply need to find our home. If we want to work on Wall Street and those jobs require clean-cut individuals, then that is our choice if we want to conform. No face tattoos or piercings? Got it. I don't believe that it is wrong for any employer to have rules and policies. Owners of businesses get to decide what employees wear and how they present themselves as a representative of the company. On the flip side, as consumers and citizens, we have the right to choose where we shop and where we apply for employment.

Maybe if I stayed wild and free, I would have become someone else, and maybe that person would not have crashed and burned at 45 years old and written a book while she put the pieces of herself back together again. Maybe that girl would have met her soul many years earlier and found her path and purpose without so much struggle, loss, and sickness.

Nah, I doubt it.

If one of my purposes was to come here on this earth to heal my childhood wounds, and if I trust in The Universe and God, then that means every single event that led me to this very moment happened exactly as it was meant to be. That means that I was not supposed to have my piercings at 22 years old, and maybe that unadorned girl is what allowed Ari and me to be taken seriously: he, as the CEO of Cumberland Farms, and me, the CEO of One Mission. I don't know if what I looked like then made a difference in how successful Cumberland or One Mission were, but what I do know is that how I felt had everything to do with my success. How I felt inside was what had me spend every waking moment working so hard to be successful; to prove I was good. Regardless of the driving emotion behind my hard work, my success was meaningful and made an impact on this world.

My success was built on feelings of not being good enough, so I powered through and pushed myself to be great (and then greater) because I wanted to be seen and heard. Every milestone hit and glass ceiling I broke through was my way of standing on the mountaintop and screaming: "Look at me! I am a good girl; I am smart and loveable. Love me, please!"

In one way, I was giving my mother the proverbial finger, saying "You can't hurt me anymore, and you certainly can't hold me back anymore." I was using the runoff of my trapped emotions as fuel to succeed and push past the labels that family had put on me; to push past the invisible hold that my mother had on me. My emotions, the ones that I would later spend years trying to release and restructure, were exactly what I needed to be me. Piercings or tattoos would not have changed my life's purpose. If I had them as I do now, they would have been part of a different façade back then.

Either way, I would have still been hiding.

The façade of the perfect wife and businesswoman was a part of my story. I don't wish to change it, and today, I am happy I discovered this part of myself. There was no other way it could have all gone down—I needed to be stripped of this part of my story to truly find out who I am on the inside. I would not have lived a freer life with more tattoos and piercings when I was younger. I was not looking to be free from what I looked like.

I was looking to be free of how I felt.

When the debacle of getting a nose ring came up with my daughters, I wanted to tell them, "You don't see it but you are already conforming to what you think people want you to be." I wanted to point out to them that they do this every time they ask me why their legs are bigger than their friend's legs, or ditch clothing they used to love because their friends don't think it is cool. They conform with every darn TikTok dance or challenge they get sucked into. I wanted to yell at them, "Nothing you do is original, you just don't see it yet. Don't be afraid to be different. One day you, too, will want to break free. You're being stifled if you continue to live by other people's standards."

The words were on the tip of my tongue: "I know it scares you that I am living outside the lines lately, but don't be afraid. I am still me, and you are still safe."

I heard Glennon Doyle's words from her book *Untamed* ringing in my ears as she once talked to her children about breaking out of their cages. Glennon left her husband and married a woman, and in her book she writes about how she felt caged for years by society and her own beliefs. She is purposefully raising her children to not live in cages. That moment, I was channeling my inner Glennon. I could see her on the side of my kitchen with pom poms: "Tell the girls you broke free from the cage of your trapped emotions. Tell them that you are no longer worried about how the world sees you because for once you finally see yourself and no longer need the approval of a woman who tortured you."

One day, both of my girls will read this book and I hope they remember this day as I do. That was the day that feelings of peace, conviction of my worth, and love for myself welled up in my heart. I had been searching for these feelings for over 10 years, and it was the idea of a nose ring and the reaction of my beautiful daughters that finally helped me find them. I loved myself and finally felt confident to be me—all in, just as I was in that very moment.

Thank you, girls. I love you.

Chapter 30
Ups and Downs

I think the hardest part of healing is that just when you think things are better and you are skipping through your day, and then—BAM, you get blindsided by a trigger. This happened to me so many times that I lost count. It still happens to me.

At the beginning of my ups and downs, I would have four or five days of being on the beam, truly feeling on point. Midway through, I could go for 30 or 45 days headache free, feeling confident and healthy, happy and free. And then, all of a sudden, I'd get washed over with anxiety like someone poured a trash barrel of ice water over my head, and the headache usually followed.

This is so disheartening when it happens because it sparks the old circuitry of fear. Why is this happening, how bad will it be, how long will it last? What will I miss while I am in this state? How will I attend this meeting or that filming? Will I feel better by the weekend? The thought-and-worry train has left the station, ladies and gentlemen. Time to hold the "oh shit handle" and ride the wave. As I've healed, I've learned to bathe in my worry rather than trying to stop it. Resistance only brings on more pain. The constriction of resistance, by definition, can't allow change to flow.

Nothing good comes from worry. Not one damn thing. If I have learned anything in my 46 years it is that worrying never makes what I am worrying about not happen. All it does is make me miserable until my brain and body realize that I am safe, and then the worry subsides. In my early 30s, I had a therapist tell me that my focus should be on getting comfortable with uncertainty, and if I did this, my anxiety would go away.

I never went back to see her, the smug little wench.

For a trauma patient, getting comfortable with uncertainty is like asking a 400-pound person to run a marathon without training. It ain't happening folks; not without major trauma healing work. She was correct in that being OK with uncertainty is a key element to living a free life, but delivery is everything. You can't simply dish out a one-liner like that to a person whose nervous system is in overdrive 24/7 and think that your comment will instantly fix them. Trauma needs to unravel, and the abused child or victim of trauma needs a voice. When the scary dark place where fear hides comes into the light, a line like "learning to live with uncertainty" can gently fall into consciousness like Forrest Gump's feather. But just saying it can't make it come to life.

It was during the COVID-19 pandemic that I had a few really bad ups and downs. Ari was not working at Cumberland Farms anymore, which was a major life change for both of us. While he was in between that and the startup of his new company, we were home together every day. The pandemic impacted marriages and relationships all over the world. I believe that it had its own consciousness, that COVID came to us to create major change in multiple ways for everyone. Ari and I went from spending the majority of our days apart while at the office, to being on top of one another all day every day.

Ari was still mourning the sale of Cumberland and was not feeling at his best. He was spending his days managing his money and buying real estate— "busy work," as he described it. Ari was built to build and create, not handle busy work each day. His frustration was building, and he often acted like a caged animal. I think he felt that way, too. Even something small, like the discussion of wearing a mask and if it was safe to attend a friend's party was just enough stress for the two of us to completely blow up and have a knock-down drag-out fight. Thanks, COVID!

As the pandemic did for the world, it also did within my marriage—it highlighted unfinished spiritual work. My PTSD around health issues ran deeper than Ari's. My mind can go from a stomach pain that has lasted a few weeks too long, to a perforated bowel that will lead to sepsis and ultimately death if we don't get to it on time. For Ari, a stomachache is simply that—a stomachache. We experienced rare scenarios with Nicholas while he was sick, and my brain stored that information and now applies it to pretty much everything in my life. COVID was no exception. For me, the virus was to be feared. I couldn't even fathom one of my children or my husband in the hospital on a ventilator.

Why did my brain automatically assume that our COVID case would end up on a ventilator? Because it was trained to think of the worst from the time I was little, and then, the worst actually did happen. Once with Nicholas, then with Evi. Two times. So, when I saw nurses making videos after their shifts on social media as they cried about how bad COVID was, I felt that sense of urgency in my body, and it triggered a fear response that was already waiting in my brain. I needed to keep my family and myself safe. That meant masks, no parties, no restaurants, and no traveling to hotels. Black and white.

COVID provided us many lessons, but the two that stand out to me are these: Ari was my mirror for the work around the PTSD from Nicholas's cancer that I had yet to process, and I was his for learning to have compassion for other people's feelings.

Ari loves to fish. We live in New England, so to fish in the off-season meant he needed to travel. Without a job to go to every day, he wanted to fish more than usual. I wanted him to fish, too—he deserved the break, and the fun! It also made sense for him to take advantage of this down time, for it would not last forever. He worked so hard, and his mind and body needed a reprieve. The only issue was that his going away to fish left me in a place that felt unsafe. Traveling meant germs, and those germs could be COVID; with every rogue thought my body was getting revved up with anxiety.

I eventually got my head around these fishing trips because I rationalized the fact that they stayed on their own boat and were contained within their small group, and they wore masks while they traveled. I was less anxious… but still anxious. When your body is in a low-level state of anxiety, it can pop at any time. So, when we got invited to a house party close to Christmas, I popped.

When we first got the invite, I thought it was going to be six couples, and one of those couples was BJ and Tiffany, whom we were already seeing. They were in our inner circle. I figured "How bad can it be? This couple has already had COVID, and we see BJ and Tiffany all the time. We will sit outside at their house, as we'll be in Florida and it will be nice outside. So, it should be safe."

The day of the party, I found out that 30 couples were invited. It was simple math for me—30 couples meant that there was no way we were going to this party. However, my husband is not that black and white. In his mind, we had already told them we were attending, and he felt bad for canceling.

"Maybe we should just go," he said to me while we sat on the beach.

The headache was looming, I could feel it. My body was feeling off, and I knew this party was going to be an issue for us. We were going to fight. "I am not going to this party," I told him. "None of us should go, it is a bad idea, and I can't believe that we are even talking about this!" I walked up to the house and poured myself a glass of wine, taking it into the pool. Surely that would help, right? Ari joined me in the pool. It may have appeared we were floating together in the water, having fun, but we were not talking and the vibe was intense.

Everyone went to the party… and we did not. We spent the night arguing instead. As with most arguments, ours didn't follow any rational path at first. Ultimately, I was able to explain to Ari that I didn't feel safe with him and his decisions. I didn't feel safe, and my brain was on autopilot, screaming for me to get out of there. "Go back to Massachusetts," my brain said. "Leave him in Florida—just get to safety." Black and white thinking.

The thing was, I didn't want to leave Florida; I wanted Ari to pick me and safety by not socializing. COVID and the party gave me a platform to ask Ari to pick me. However, most people are not mind readers, and usually we need to ask for what we want. I needed to tell Ari that I needed him to pick me. Pick me over work, pick me over COVID; choose to fight for me and protect me. But I hated every second that I had to ask him for these things. I felt weak and pathetic.

Why did I feel that way? Feelings of vulnerability brought out The Protector, who thought being vulnerable was weak and pathetic. The Protector thought that the soft and kind Ashley was weak and pathetic to need our mother's love. It was that argument with Ari when it hit me; I mean, *really* hit me: Ari is not my mother. It is safe to love him, and he needs me to be explicit with him about my needs. I can ask him for what I need, and it does not make me weak or pathetic. In fact, it makes me strong, and the bonus? I get what I want!

It took us four hours of talking, but we got there. What a gift Ari is to me. He is so willing to meet me where I am broken, and he listens and is articulate about what he needs and how he feels. This is what must have made him a great CEO—he can listen while keeping what was said in order in his head without emotion, then organize it in a way that makes sense in the end for a perfect solution. I believe his superpower is his dedication to me and our marriage. He stands firm until the end. When I usually try to flee, he stands his ground tall and strong, all the while showing me that he is safe to be with.

For me, the work will never be done. I used to see everything in my life—including spiritual and emotional growth—as something I could check off my list. I was a "get things done" girl, never leaving tasks on my list. If that meant I worked all night, then that is what I did. I even looked at therapy as a task I could complete.

> Discussed mother's abuse today in therapy, CHECK.
> Talked about the argument I had with my husband last night, CHECK.

As if just talking about my life's circumstances was all I needed to do for it to be all better. I couldn't have been more wrong. Talking about our story is a good first step, but staying there and not incorporating any tools that help you to release the story—to connect the dots on where the feelings originated, or use tools that help to calm your nervous system down—is just talking in circles, and it never helped me all that much.

Today, when I discuss an argument with my husband, I unpack it in a way that calms my brain down and gives me the ability to see my triggers, connect where they came from, and then release them. For example, when I told Anna about the house party and our argument about not going, our discussion went something like this: "Ari and I had a big blow out last night. We got invited to a party that I didn't want to go to, because I thought it was too risky from a COVID perspective. So, we basically ignored each other most of the day, and when it came down to the final moment we had to decide if we were going, it all blew up."

As I stopped to take a breath, ready to continue telling my story, Anna stopped me and asked if we could pause. "I am wondering, Ashley, how your body is feeling right now. Can we check in with that?"

As I always do, I said yes and closed my eyes. Anna walked me through feeling the seat under my body, relaxing my shoulders and slowing my breath. "Now," she said, "where in your body do you feel tension?"

"My neck, back, and forehead," I replied.

"Good. Tell me, Ashley, what is the emotion behind those areas of tension? What is coming up for you?"

"I am scared, angry, and I feel alone," I said. "I feel like something bad is going to happen."

"You are scared, good. Tell me what you are scared about."

"I don't feel safe."

"Tell me about that. Why do you not feel safe?"

"If we go to this party, we have no idea where the other guests have been, or if they wear masks when they are out, and if they don't, we could get COVID. It just isn't safe," I said, then paused.

"Tell me about feeling alone, Ashley," Anna said softly.

"I just don't understand why Ari can't hear my pleas," I said. "Why does he not want to make decisions that keep our family safe?"

"Your mind is telling you that you feel unsafe right now about getting COVID, but can you tell me if there is any other reason your brain and body feel unsafe?" Anna asked.

"Well, I don't feel too safe in my own house right now, either."

"Tell me more about that."

"I feel like my husband is making bad decisions. I feel like he isn't listening to me; I feel like we are not on the same page, and I am angry. All of that feels unsafe to me."

This is the part of our conversations when Anna usually helps me to make connections. We identified that there were two situations in my life that were causing my brain to think that it was unsafe, but the bottom line was that I was angry, and I wasn't allowing myself to be angry. It wasn't natural for me to be in touch with the part of me that wanted to say, "Ari, I am angry that you are not making decisions for the safety of our family." My brain wouldn't let me get in touch with the emotion of anger. Instead, it gave me a headache to protect me from experiencing anger.

Most children who lived in abusive homes as I did never had permission to be angry. I certainly did not. As we grow into adults, we form opinions about when it is appropriate to express our anger, and for a woman, that is almost never. The confusion of feeling one way on the inside and putting forth a different expression on the outside causes pain and suffering.

For me, the triggers were feeling out of control in my environment—the conflict over to go or not go to the party—and also feeling unheard—Ari not listening to me about why we should have stayed home. Both of these situations were triggering an old fear response from my childhood. My mother never listened to me. In fact, it was quite the opposite. When I did talk about my feelings, she gaslighted me. She undermined, invalidated, and scoffed at me every time. Although this situation was not the exact same one as when I was a child, my brain didn't know the difference. Unsafe is unsafe, and that means "go into lockdown and do whatever you need to do to claw your way to safety."

In the present moment, I actually was safe. Ari and I decided not to go to the party, but simply taking that off the list of things to worry about was not enough for me to decide to feel safe. It was too late, and my fear circuits were firing out of control. The same concept applies to Ari not hearing and ignoring me when I expressed concern about why we shouldn't go to the party. Although we were talking by the end of the night, the trigger had already happened, and my brain and body were mounting a response. The emotions had come up, and now they needed to be dealt with in order for me to calm down again.

The gift my husband gave to me in that moment was his ability to talk about why we both ignored one another all day. I'm thankful that he can easily give voice to feelings of hurt, anger, and judgment. After my discussion with Ari, I laid down for 30 minutes and focused on my breath. In and out. I even said those words out loud: "in" on my inhale and "out" on my exhale. I did this gently and easily until I felt my body calm down, my heart rate decrease, and my body feel less tense.

It usually takes me a few days to fully reach baseline after a big event like an argument or large crowded party. Historically, I never gave myself that time to recuperate, I just pushed on piling more stress on top of stress. It was the opposite of self-care.

Now, I actually block time in my calendar the day before and day after a big event, and if I have an unforeseen event happen like an argument, I will reschedule meetings and calls the next day, if possible, to give my body time to settle down. I choose to do this for myself because I know it is what my body needs to heal. I resisted this part of self-care for years because I saw the act of slowing down as weak, and subconsciously, I felt like if I acknowledged the pain, then it would be real. By making self-care a priority, it changed everything for me. I am healthier, and I have more feelings of safety and control over my emotions. Before, I was always searching for the pot of gold at the end of the rainbow, thinking I would be happy *if* and *when* something happened. I didn't understand that happiness was already inside me and that it was my responsibility to connect to it. I was able to do this as I found my way to feelings of safety. Living a task-oriented life and always planning for a state of happiness in the future, stopped me from enjoying the rainbow for what it was; the journey. It is all about the journey, never just about the pot of gold.

Before I got to this point in my healing, I laid on the table of at least 10 really powerful healers, looking to them to fix me. I have been ready to heal so many times in my life, but I saw the healer as the one with the power to heal me, not myself. I went into every session thinking I was being a good patient, giving my body permission to open up to the gift of the energy that each of them gave me. However, it simply wasn't enough to make the big change I was looking for, because I believed that the healing came from an outside source. I had to become an active participant in my own healing.

The road to get to that realization was full of some pretty amazing experiences, and I will share a few of them with you in the following chapters. What I have come to understand is that collectively, each healer I went to and class I took was prepping my mind and body for the deep work I would eventually do with Anna. In short, it all unfolded exactly as it was supposed to, and I am grateful that I finally came to the realization that I had the power to make the healing changes in my life. My healing came from deep within me, not at the hands of others.

Chapter 31
Breaking Free

I see the past in the eyes of everyone I meet. But I couldn't always do this. For years, I took everything at face value, thinking when someone yelled at me in traffic that he was an angry asshole, or if a friend betrayed me she was simply a bad person. As I untangled my past trauma and was able to see how and where it was showing up in my everyday life, I began seeing everyone as a tangled mess of their own past trauma. I have often said that everyone could benefit from therapy, and I add to that today by saying everyone could benefit from healing the wounds of their inner child.

Somewhere in the weeds of writing this book, I was at acupuncture, not feeling well. I had not been to treatment in months due to the pandemic, and I was feeling heavy with emotions. My body was unbalanced. Acupuncture continues to be an amazing tool for my body to release and heal. If I go weeks—or in this case, months—without it, I feel the buildup of stagnant energy in my body. My muscles tighten, I'm fatigued, and my head is foggy. But when someone asks me how I am, even if I feel like I am dying, I say, "I am good, and how are you?"

When Robert, my acupuncturist, asked me how I had been feeling these past few months, I replied, "Good!" I was far from good, but I hate to burden people with my junk. I kept it simple. I told him that I was writing a book, and I was finding it difficult to relive the trauma again. After he placed the needles in what seemed like everywhere, he told me to breathe deeply down into my belly. "Do a meditation," he said. "I know you love that stuff." Then he promptly left the room.

As the good little girl does, I followed instructions. *Meditate. Got it.* I began to breathe deeply and let go. I followed my personal primordial sound mantra that had been given to me in my Chopra Center meditation class, and I was off deep into the space between my thoughts. The next thing I knew, I was distracted by the thought that going to my childhood home may be in order as a healing moment. As soon as I had that idea, I quickly figured out that it would be impossible to show up at a stranger's house and say, "Hi, sorry to bother you, but I grew up in this house, and I am processing some abuse and would love to walk around and cry a little in your house. Is that cool?"

Yeah, that wasn't going to work. Within my very next thought, I saw myself at the front door, and I heard a voice that said, "You can go there now." This sound came to me just like the low bellow of a voice that told me to get a Lyme test so many years earlier.

There I stood, in my mind's eye, at the aqua blue front door of my childhood home. *What am I doing here?* I thought. Then I felt a tiny soft hand that gently fit into mine. I looked down and saw myself; I was 5 years old. This little girl looked terrified. We walked inside, and I got down on my knees to talk to her.

Me, at age 45 said, "Mom is gone. She is dead now, and she can't hurt us anymore."

Age 5: "Are you sure?"

Age 45: "Yes, I promise. Go ahead and look around. She is gone."

The 5-year-old me hesitantly walked through the one-level home, slowly going into all the rooms. She went from her bedroom into Mom's, looking at me with wide eyes.

Age 5: "She isn't here. She is gone; really gone."

Age 45: "Yes, she is gone."

The little girl walked into the living room, then the kitchen, and with each step, she began to walk faster and faster while her face became less tense. We met halfway between the kitchen and the den, and she fell into my lap crying and grasping onto me.

Age 45: "She is gone, and we are safe now. We are safe now. We don't have to worry anymore that something bad is going to happen. The monster is gone."

Then we just cried together.

The little girl broke free from our embrace with a hopeful and passionate look and said to me, "Oh my God, we have to tell the others. They all need to know that she is gone."

Age 45: "Yes, of course. Let's go tell the others."

We called a meeting and invited all of the other child parts of me that were abused by our mother to come and sit in our circle. I knew then that the little girl I had with me was The Terrified One. Whenever I was terrified in my adult life, it was this little girl who got triggered. She came forward and altered my thinking to head straight for all of the bad possible outcomes. I recognized her now; she was with me a lot. What she was asking us to do was call forward all of the others: The Angry Me, The Responsible Me, The Ashamed, The Protector, The Sad Me, and so on. There were so many parts of me that showed up, all there to tell me their story.

We formed a circle and instantly my childhood living room was full of me in so many different ages and stages of my life, from 5 to 30 years old. I could see the anger on their faces, the sadness, the terror—all of it. It was as if I was watching a movie of my life, and all of the characters were standing right in front of me. The Terrified One stood up and held my hand, and then I made an announcement.

Age 45: "Ashley wanted me to call this meeting because she learned something today that she wants to tell you."

The little girl stood tall and cleared her throat like she was going to make the most amazing announcement ever.

Age 5: "Mom is gone, she is dead."

The crowd began talking to each other, looking for answers. Some of the faces were stoic, others began smiling.

Age 5: "We are safe now. We are safe now. She can't hurt us anymore."

Then a light began to shine on the face of one little girl in the back of the crowd. She was not having it; she didn't believe what we were telling her. She didn't trust that Mom was gone. She identified herself as The Scared One.

She told us her story, about how it felt to see Mom pull into the driveway after work as she worried about what kind of mood she would be in. She explained how she would try to prepare for the nights Mom was angry and would be mad at her by making sure the house was clean and organized, and then retreating to her room. But that didn't always work, and she didn't know why. She never seemed to get it right. She went on to explain her fear when she heard Mom walk down the hallway, afraid that she would come into her room and yell at her for something. She told us how she was always scared. At school, when she was away from Mom, she was still scared about going home.

We all listened quietly to her story, and when she finished, another little girl came forward and stood next to The Scared One. She told us she was The Protector, and shared about how she spent her days and nights trying to protect all of us from our mother. She told us that she was the one who came up with plans on how to clean the house and arrange the furniture, and she taught us how to act, all in hopes of trying to make things just right so it would make Mom happy and she wouldn't yell or scream.

The Protector was also very angry at our mother, for all of us. She was tired; tired of having to protect us all these years against mother's rage, and there was no place to release this angst. She hated Mom for what she did to us, and learned to hide her anger as a protection mechanism. Expressing anger was just another way to get into trouble in our house. This went on and on.

One by one, little children, teenagers, and young adults all came forward to tell us their stories. The Abandoned One came forward and let it all out: "She would never talk to me when I needed her to; she would throw my letters to her back at me and walk away. When I broke my leg, she left me waiting for hours before she took me to the hospital. When I needed stitches for a deep cut I got at school, she refused to take me to the hospital because she said she was tired. She left us. She left us and moved to Florida. She left us at our wedding; she left us when Nicholas was sick. She was always leaving us, and it is so, so, sad. I am so sad. Why didn't she love us? What did we do to make her not love us?"

I felt all of what they were saying. The feelings and emotions were so real, and my heart was opening up to them in such a profound way. I was feeling! And I was still alive. Feeling wasn't killing me. In fact, I actually liked it.

Age 45: "I am so honored that all of you came forward today. Each of you has a very important story to tell, and I want you to know that I want to hear it. I am here to listen to you, and I love you all. Please be patient with me; I promise to get to each of you in time. I may need to take breaks here and there because this is heavy stuff. Please be patient with me; we will do the work together. We will heal together."

It was a healing circle of epic proportions. All the emotions came forward that day in acupuncture. I don't know how long I was in the room, but when the doorknob clicked, I was clear-headed and wiping tears off my cheeks. As I drove home that day, it all made perfect sense. This was the work that I had been doing with Anna. We were getting to the emotions I had been pushing deep down since childhood, and today, they all came forward.

This experience was life-changing for me, and everything I was wrestling with was becoming clear. I met all of the parts of me that still needed healing. I knew that until I began to heal the parts of me that were abused, I would be triggered by the world around me over and over again.

This is the work: to observe yourself in life. To see how reactions and emotions come up and relate them back to unresolved issues, circumstances, and emotions.

I am obviously not perfect, and I don't catch myself every time. Still, more often than not, nowadays I stop myself and ask, "Am I being triggered right now?" If the answer is yes, then I journal it out. I also have more capacity for accepting people now. I have the ability to pause before I react, and I can see an aura around people that tells me, "Ah yes, this is a childhood wound for them, and this is why they are acting this way."

Meditation and journaling work to heal my inner child were what got me back on my feet after my collapse into migraines. These were what helped me write this book. If you are ready to heal, I encourage you to just take the first step of a meditation practice. Let this ancient healing method help and guide you on your path. You will figure out the rest as you go, and the space you create in your mind through meditation will help you make decisions, listen to your gut instinct, and calm your nervous system down in order to get the most out of whatever healing modality you choose to use.

If you are overwhelmed with this notion, go to my website! I have a bunch of resources for you to listen to and watch at ashleyhaseotes.com.

Chapter 32
Atlas Bone

*B*efore I found Pedro and ultimately began working with Anna, I would have tried anything to feel better—and try I did. As I lay on the table of yet another healer just a few months before my collapse into migraines, I prayed desperately for answers. She was cradling my head in her hands, and I was deep in relaxation when she told me she knew why I was having migraines.

"Your atlas bone, the first cervical spine vertebra, is off, Ashley. It makes an important connection with the base of your skull, the occipital bone. You need to find a chiropractor who can adjust it for you. This will solve all of your issues with headaches and vertigo."

I had no idea that my atlas and occipital bones even existed, let alone that they could be off kilter. Obviously, I went straight home and immediately consulted Dr. Google. Just as the healer had suggested, I had all the symptoms of this misalignment. So, I found a chiropractor that did just this precise adjustment and scheduled an appointment. Not all chiropractors will adjust your atlas, as it is a specialty within the chiropractic world.

A few days later, I sat in the waiting room filled with anxiety. Would it work? Would adjustment make it worse? How can I trust this guy? My mind was racing. I mean, I was borderline panicking. How I missed this red flag that my body was giving me, I have no idea. It was like the feeling you would get right before you were to walk into an abandoned house with your friends at 10 years old when everything in you is screaming, "Don't go in!"

We get these gut punches for a reason, but for years, I ignored mine. I pushed the warning signs aside as fear, and I forged on. The funny thing is, at the time, I thought I was winning! I celebrated pushing aside my feelings of panic as an accomplishment of conquering my fear. Except this time it wasn't fear, it actually was my body saying, "This isn't right for us—don't go in!" It was always difficult for me to distinguish between gut instinct and fear because my life was so fear-driven for so long. It took doing this work for a few years before I could trust my body signals again.

I met a few nice patients in the waiting room, and they all seemed thrilled with this doctor and told me it was going to change my life. Each time I spoke with yet another person in his waiting room, I began to relax, thinking that perhaps this was going to be my key to getting my life back. He took me back, did an hour's worth of X-rays and then told me to come back in a week for the results. Indeed, my atlas and occipital bones were misaligned, as well as many other issues with my spine and neck.

Now, it is important to note here that there are many people walking around right now with bulging discs, bad scoliosis, and other misalignments, and they are not in pain nor do they need corrective surgery. I didn't learn the concept that not everything that looks broken actually is broken until I began the work with Curable.

The doctor told me that he was shocked I had gone on as long as I had with this large of a misalignment, and, cue drum roll—he was going to fix me. The protocol was a pinpoint hammer-like adjustment after which I had to lie very still for 15 minutes before I could leave his office. This was yet another thing that had me questioning this whole thing. Why did I have to lay there super still on the table? If I moved, what would happen? Would I sever a nerve and become paralyzed? What was this adjustment doing to my body? Additionally, I was instructed to move my neck like I was in a brace for a week after the adjustment. No quick turns or looking side to side.

A tiny voice inside my head kept saying, "This doesn't feel right." The adjustment itself was a piece of cake. Shocking, but easy. I laid on my side as he found the exact angle per my X-rays to align the tool that was going to give my atlas bone the adjustment. Picture a stamping machine used to adhere logos to a piece of clothing, except this was a fine-pointed tool. It took all of one minute, and I was done. I survived.

I drove home feeling great. In talking to my employees, I described that, for once, I actually felt both of my feet on the ground at the exact same time. I was convinced this was my ticket to feeling better.

Until I woke up the next day with vertigo, and boy was it back with a vengeance.

During this time, I was in denial that anything was severely wrong with me, so I carried on. I took Nicholas to the orthodontist, and the whole time I was there I could feel the earth moving underneath me. I was starting to get anxious because I had a day booked full of meetings for One Mission, and I was worried that I wouldn't be able to get through them with the world moving and shifting underneath me.

As I drove to the office, I could tell that something just wasn't right. My vision was off, and my whole body ached in pain. I did my very best to get through the meetings, but I was visibly uncomfortable and agitated. I should have just gone home, but back then, I didn't take care of myself like that. As I started my last call with my media partner, I couldn't even stand up straight. I called the chiropractor and told him what was going on, and he told me that this can happen and that I should come in to see him right away. I never made it to his office. I had one of the worst vertigo episodes I have ever had in my life as I drove down the highway alone.

The pressure in my head came to a screeching impact. It was like a downward pressure coming from above my body pushing me with such a force that I could not escape it. My vision went dark and I could barely lift my arms. I felt like I was on a roller coaster and my arms were floating within the denseness of gravity. I put on my blinker and prayed to God I would make it to the side of the road without crashing. I couldn't see anything, not even my phone. Thank God for Siri, because that is how I called for help.

Though many people get relief from this adjustment, I did not. In fact, I am convinced that it made me worse. This was the beginning of my steep downward spiral with worsening migraines and vertigo.

Do you find yourself doctor hopping and searching for a quick fix? Are you coming up short, never finding the answers you're looking for?

I want to challenge you that perhaps the answers to your pain are not "out there." Perhaps they are well within your own body—you just have to be open to looking for them there.

Chapter 33
Craniosacral Therapy

A few weeks before I found Pedro, and after the circus of my atlas-occipital bone adjustments, I woke up to another headache, more anxiety, and still no answers. So, I booked an appointment with an orthopedic surgeon at Newton Wellesley Hospital. I figured at this point if my back, occipital bone, and neck were really that off and causing me this much discomfort, I would consider surgery. As surgeons do, he ordered an MRI, and more X-rays. At this point, I think my body glows from all the radiation from these tests!

As I waited for my follow-up appointment with the surgeon, I was still desperately searching, looking outward for the answers. I saw myself as a problem that needed fixing. I was thinking the issue was within my physical body—that was what was broken. I stood next to the surgeon in his blue scrubs, looking at my X-ray. "Is my occipital bone misaligned?" I asked him, hoping he would see what the chiropractor saw on his X-rays.

"Nope," he said quickly. "Everything looks fine to me. I don't see anything on this X-ray that would lead to dizziness, headaches, or vertigo. Congrats, you're in good working order!"

I was relieved... but confused. One doctor tells me I have such a misalignment that there is no wonder why I have vertigo, and the other doesn't see a thing wrong. I didn't know what to believe, and I still didn't have any answers. I would have consulted a homeless person on the street at this point if I thought I would find the answer. Feeling hopeless, I went back to yet another healer.

This time I was referred to a body worker who does craniosacral therapy. I asked my friend Google "What is craniosacral therapy?"—also known as CST—and this is what I found:

> [CST] is a gentle hands-on technique that uses a light touch to examine membranes and movement of the fluids in and around the central nervous system. Relieving tension in the central nervous system promotes a feeling of well-being by eliminating pain and boosting health and immunity.[1]

Sounded gentle enough for me, so I made an appointment. I instantly loved my practitioner—she was gentle and kind. Even at my first appointment, I wasn't anxious in the slightest bit. In fact, it was just the opposite: I trusted her completely. The most interesting part about my first session was that I found myself in a church parking lot just down the street from her office, with only 20 minutes to spare before my appointment. This was the church that my grandfather worked at when I was young, and it was also the church in which I held my mother's funeral. I found an open door and walked straight into the church and sat down in a pew. The memory of giving my mother's eulogy came flooding in.

I recalled the discussion I had with my Uncle Steve a few days after my mother died. He insisted that I give her eulogy, and I tried to tell him that he should give it because I didn't really have much in the way of good things to say about her. Weirdly, I felt both like it was my duty as her daughter to speak, but also I got the feeling that no one else wanted to. That part of the death of my mother, the planning for her funeral and speakers at the church service, was such a blur. I simply took my uncle's lead, and figured that now he knew the true story of me and my mother, but still wanted me to speak, it must be fate.

Sitting again in the church, I could feel everything in my body from the moment I stood at the pulpit to give my mother's eulogy. My heart was beating so rapidly I could hear it in my ears. I began by saying "My mother and I had a difficult relationship. In fact, we stopped talking the

---

[1]https://my.clevelandclinic.org/health/treatments/17677-craniosacral-therapy

day I got married..." then I blacked out. I don't remember a single thing I said after those opening words. Just thinking about that day brought me to a screaming cry as I sat in the empty church, and I was wailing so loudly I didn't care if anyone heard me. I got on my knees and prayed, "God please help me heal from the wounds I carry at the hands of my mother. Please help me."

I stood up, splashed holy water on my face, left a donation with the secretary (who was looking at my tear-streamed face and puffy red eyes with worry), and drove down the street to my appointment.

It was no accident that her office was just one block from that church. It was no accident that I was on my knees asking God for help, and then only minutes later, I was energetically open to his healing.

CST that day was amazing. It pulled out old dark memories that I had forgotten about, and I found it extremely relaxing and deeply excavating. I felt lighter when I left her office, but the next day, I got another migraine.

Looking back, I was unearthing deeply buried emotions through all of these healing sessions, and my body was too fragile for it. I should have been in therapy while I was going to all these healers, as it would have been a safe place to process what was coming up. Rather, I would go to a healer, dig up a ton of old buried emotions, and then try to go back to life as if nothing happened; thinking that the un-earthing was the work. But it wasn't. I needed more.

The unearthing in and of itself was re-traumatizing my nervous system; not healing it, as I had hoped. What I needed was trauma therapy. Trauma therapy is unique, and often at the beginning, the therapist won't have you talk at all about what happened. Instead, they focus on nervous system regulation and helping the mind to feel safe. Usually this is done through somatic exercises such as breathing techniques, sensation awareness, massage, and other body work.

I only ended up doing this work after *years* of re-traumatization.

You want to do everything you can to protect yourself from re-traumatization, which can happen very easily if you are not careful during your healing. I had to create a team of people to help me heal and made sure they were all on the same page with what was happening with me. I used my voice, advocated for myself, set boundaries, and did the work. My team was small—it included Anna, Ari, my massage therapist Kristen, a few trusted friends, my acupuncturist Robert, and my beloved Lucinda.

Massage and acupuncture were key for me. However, many people forget how powerful these modalities are at moving energy and opening up both physical and emotional blockages in our bodies. As I am very sensitive to both acupuncture and massage, I made sure to talk about what was coming up for me—in the moment, as it happened—with both Robert and Kristen. This communication was crucial to keeping me feeling safe in their hands. Feeling safe is how I healed, as my brain would not and could not have benefitted from the work without feeling protected and secure with my team of people.

To make sure I was continually feeling safe, there were practical tools I utilized along the way. For example, I would ask Robert why he was doing certain treatments and shared how my body felt afterward. This way I participated rather than feeling like treatment was just being done to me by the hands of someone else. Robert's discussing his thought process of treatment with me, and getting my input, created safety for my brain and body. Ultimately, this allowed the treatment to enter in my energy field easily and effortlessly for my highest healing good.

With Kristen, I was open about my trauma, and she played a huge part in my healing. I trusted her to keep herself healthy, so that she was best able to help my body release old energy. Then we both let go of the heaviness together. Massage therapists are hands-on healers, and you want to make sure that yours is taking good care of themselves, which will allow your body a safe and energetically clean place to heal and release.

This may sound like a small thing, but even being able to move around during the massage was hugely helpful during my healing. Trauma victims freeze, and even years later, our instinct is to freeze when we get triggered. Together, she and I came up with a plan where I would move my body if and when any anxiety popped up, or I simply felt the need to move. Making the choice to move if I felt the need to during a massage sent messages to my brain, giving the message that it was safe, and that I was in charge of the present moment.

Reminding our primitive brain, the childhood brain, that we are safe is the name of the game when healing trauma. Everything that I did, people that I hung around with, places I went, food I ate, what I watched, and what I read—everything was aimed at safety. Over time, my brain got the message: I was safe.

Having a team of people supporting me in my new way of living, focused on safety, was key to my success.

My advice to you as you embark or continue on your journey is this: Ask yourself if what you are doing is making you feel better or worse. Are you seeing major changes in your life that you can attribute to the work you are doing? If not, maybe it is time to try a new method. Maybe you, too, are re-traumatizing yourself with the methods you are using.

How do you know when to move on? The simple answer is you will intuitively know when the time is right. The not-so-simple answer is that everything takes time, so don't ditch too early, but don't overstay when it isn't working either. If you would prefer to do the healing energetically, make sure that you have a coach or a teacher you can have regular one-on-one sessions with to process your trauma. If I had done that, I may not have crashed and burned—who knows.

Chapter 34
Not All Pain Is Equal

*A*ssuming you are like me, and your doctors are telling you that there is nothing wrong with you, then your chronic pain is otherwise known as neuroplastic pain. This is a mind/body issue.

But how do you know if your pain is being caused by your brain? An easy way to test this out is to notice if your pain is only present some of the times you do the same activity. If you walk to the mailbox every afternoon, and on Monday your pain is an 8 out of 10, but on Thursday when you take that same walk the pain drops to a 3 out of 10, it could be neuroplastic pain. Or, if your pain moves around—for instance, sometimes it is in your left foot and then other days it is in the right foot—it could be neuroplastic as well. Another huge indicator that your pain is neuroplastic is if it started after a big life event, or if you can trace it to emotional stress.

Neuroplastic pain is real pain, but it is due to a false alarm created in your brain. It is your brain creating pain where there is no real physical issue because it feels unsafe. If the word unsafe seems too touchy-feely for you, you can replace it with overworked, overburdened, or completely stressed out. All of these are also feelings of not being safe.

You may identify with feeling over-worked. What lies underneath that feeling? Ask yourself what you are afraid of, if you don't work that hard. Is there an underlying fear about not having enough money? Are you afraid of not being seen as important? Or, are you trying to prove your worth to yourself to someone? Usually, our negative feelings are driven by a fear of not having our needs met.

Unfortunately, fear is the fuel for the pain. It quite literally keeps the pain alive. In chronic pain sufferers, however, our fear about our pain is falsely labeled, because the fear is usually about other things: fear of failure, fear of abandonment, fear of not being worthy or good enough, fear of not having a voice.

In this book, I have (hopefully) clearly laid out my mind-body connection, and you can see that my fear responses were the source of my pain. In order for me to break the pain cycle, I had to break the fear cycle.

If you are questioning if your pain is neuroplastic pain, try the Google!

Being able to finally stop trying to figure out what was physically wrong with my body was where I started this journey of getting my life back. If you have neuroplastic pain, like me, you must be willing to admit that your problem is emotional, not physical.

For me, I knew for sure my pain was neuroplastic because after I had a glass of wine, my pain would decrease or even go away at times. Many neuroplastic pain patients also have a history that includes years of weird symptoms.

Here is mine: Beginning in my 20s, I had bouts of lower pelvic pain that went on for 6 years, urinary symptoms, and side pain that never left after I popped a rib out. I complained of earaches, "full" feeling ears, and facial pain that was not a sinus infection. I had stomachaches that went on for days and had hip and back pain that left me unable to walk and exercise.

I was in and out of the doctor's office, off and on antibiotics, and eventually, my doctor gave me Ativan to help me sleep. That was nearly my demise.

Ativan is very addictive, both mentally and physically. I didn't know it at the time, and my doctor never talked to me about it. A bottle would last me more than a month, so I guess by definition I didn't have a problem. I was on a very low dose, and I usually only took it if my anxiety was stopping me from sleeping. I would take it for a few days then stop.

While I was in treatment with Pedro, we discovered that I was having withdrawal symptoms and I had to find a psychiatrist to help me wean off. It was a nightmare; weaning off was needed even for a low dose of .25 mg. Coming off Ativan is like having a million spiders inside your body trying to get out while, at the same time, you are unable to control the thoughts running through your head. My anxiety was off the charts and completely out of control. I cried almost every day for hours during this process.

I will never ever take Ativan again.

Another healer who helped to bring me back after my collapse into migraines was Rob Wergin. I have experienced many healings throughout my years, but none quite like Rob Wergin. I found his work after watching the "Heal" documentary on Netflix in 2019. Kelly Gores produced this documentary as she was fascinated with how and why people became ill and why miracles happen to some people and not others. Her documentary takes people on a scientific and spiritual journey where they discover that their thoughts, beliefs, and emotions have a significant impact on their health and ability to heal.

The latest science reveals that we are not victims of unchangeable genes, nor should we buy into a scary prognosis. The fact is we have more control over our health and life than we have been taught to believe. This film will empower you with a new understanding of the miraculous nature of the human body and the extraordinary healer within us all.

She interviews Deepak Chopra, Dr. Joe Dispenza, Rob Wergin, and more. It is a wonderful introduction to what is out there for modalities for people to try in their local area… or you could do what I did and just use Rob Wergin! This documentary brought me feelings of togetherness with others who are suffering, and most importantly, it brought me hope that indeed I could once again feel whole.

Because of the "Heal" documentary, I have been working with Rob for almost two years now. I have released some heavy energy in my body, leaving me feeling lighter and more energetic. I feel closer to God than ever before, and I recommend Rob to everyone who asks me for a good healer.

Recovery is not a straight line. You do not start off sick or suffering, begin the work, and continue to compound your progress so that it ultimately leads you through the rainbow and to the pot of gold.

I know, I know. This is disappointing. Trust me, I get it. I wish that healing was simple math. I wish you could check off the boxes. I wish you could wake up sick, gather the numbers, and then the next day begin to add them together and boom—you have an answer.

My healing was and continues to look more like a waitress working in a very fast-paced busy restaurant. A good waitress always walks around in circles, juggling five different table orders, sides, accoutrements, stacking glasses, filling ice bins, and grabbing ketchup bottles. It is a balancing act.

Healing from my migraines looks just like that.

On the outside, everyone thinks I am better because I have left my couch and am back in the world again. But what many people don't know is that I am still juggling. They don't know that I am still in the weeds, working my way through the forest of triggers and emotions and trying to pave new pathways in my brain through which I can then walk and not feel so triggered.

Does this mean I am migraine-free? Definitely not. I have taken huge strides from where I was, yes, and to most people that looks like a straight line… but it isn't. I still have days where I don't want to leave the house, or days where my anxiety is off the charts and I can't answer the phone when it rings. I still get headaches. But I don't get debilitating migraines that leave me bedridden, and my pain is shifting and changing, which means that it is on its way out.

I have plenty of pain-free days, and then I have weeks when I am dealing with a headache every day. On these days, I rest my mind and my body. I literally lie down during the day and rest, which is something I would have never done before, unless I was physically unable to stand up and push on—if I literally couldn't make it to the office.

I had to get comfortable with allowing my chronic pain to unfold, piece by piece. If the timeline was that my trauma began when I was five, and my pain began when I was in my twenties, then I can't expect that just because I uncovered the cause of my pain, it will disappear without the element of time. I will be pain-free at some point, I trust and know that. In the meantime, I am happy to put in the work needed each day for that to happen.

Healing is personal, and time is relative to each person. We are not supposed to duplicate other people's healing journeys; we are simply to chart our own journey and share it with others to inspire them on their own journey. Through these pages, I've shared how I healed to help you regain the hope for healing that may feel impossibly far off.

Maybe you can take a few things from my toolbox that felt good for you and try them on for yourself. The journaling techniques I use are heavily based on Nichole Sachs, LICSW, Dr. John Sarno, and The Curable App, which you can look up online. I also have free mediations on my website for you to try at ashleyhaseotes.com. I've also made "The Meeting of the Children" from my acupuncture session available for you to download there. Try it out and see what child parts of you would like to share their story.

Ultimately, your healing journey will look different than mine, as your suffering is unique to you. Keep the faith, and remember, any forward progress is good. It will pay off in the end. You most likely don't know where your end is yet, but it will all make sense when you get there. All you need is faith the size of a mustard seed!

You may be inspired after reading this to begin the work, or to take your healing journey to the next level. I applaud you, and cheer for you. Let your life unfold, let your emotions talk to you, and let your body release and exhale. Learn to see your struggles as the lessons they are intended to be. Loosen your grip ever so gently on the outcome, accept the process, and effortlessly take your next step. It is your destiny to return home to your soul; the place where everything feels right and makes sense.

Lastly, seek to remember that you chose this life and all its experiences. It is in the journey where you will find the most rewarding parts of life; not in reaching the destination.

Chapter 35
Don't Fight It

*A*s I came to the close of writing this book, a friend of mine asked me to talk with her teenage son. He was having terrible panic attacks, they felt like they had tried everything to help him, and nothing was working.

So, I offered to help.

This young man had just ended an abusive relationship with his best friend; he was using drugs and ditched therapy. A recipe for a panic attack, if you ask me. One day when we were on Zoom, I asked him, "Do you believe in God?"

"I guess so," he responded.

I told him that it was important for him to believe in some type of higher power. It was going to be a crucial part of his healing journey to believe that he came from a source of energy that was larger than he, and for him to understand that he shares this energy with all of humanity.

"You need to know that you are not alone in this crazy world," I told him. I walked him through my own beliefs and asked him if any of it resonated with him.

"God created me as his child so that he could experience the world through me. We are all his children. He put me on earth, but prior to that, together we agreed upon what my human life would be. He never set out for me to suffer," I told him, "And the same is true for you."

"So why do we suffer?" he asked.

I paused before sharing my answer. "I believe we suffer when we are in resistance to the energy and flow of our lives. We are in resistance when we are not connected with our soul, our purpose, and with God. We all have a purpose for living, and perhaps the experiences we face are opportunities to learn and evolve our soul. This is a natural process. It hurts when we fight it or are unable to learn from it. This resistance is a very common human trait; this suffering is something we all share. But suffering is not our destiny. The growth and evolution from our life circumstances is what our destiny ultimately is. Allow what happened in your life to be, allow it in. It happened to you, but it is not who you are. Don't fight it and don't hold onto it. Try to unfold your power into the fabric of the details of your life, but don't see them as bad, just see them for what they are—fabrics of your story, not the whole you."

These words, what I believe to be the words of God came to me as easily as breathing. Perhaps because I was on the tail end of a life lesson myself and finally understood how my own resistance had caused me to suffer. I taught him how to journal out the voices of the emotions that he was trying so hard to hold in. Together we let his life unfold, and we let God in.

Believing in a source higher than myself was and continues to be how I heal. I will not tell you that you must believe in God or hold the same beliefs about God as I do in order to heal. I don't believe there is a one-size-fits-all approach to healing, nor is it required for you to believe in God. I know a very smart woman who on her healing journey called God "spoon," because she was not totally on board with believing in the Big Guy. You will find your source of healing that works perfectly for you. The only thing that you can do is to believe in and trust in the process.

Epilogue

*O*nly a few short weeks prior to the printing of this book, I was on a beach in Florida looking out at the ocean when it hit me—I wrote a book. I wrote a freaking book!

In that very moment, as the ocean water tickled my feet, my whole body was washed over in what I can only describe to you as a sensation of both anxiety and calm in the same moment. *Is it even possible to be anxious and at peace in the same moment? Because that is what just happened...*

As with every other anxiety attack, a wave of prickles and simultaneous heat flooded my chest and face. But what happened in this moment was that I *observed* the emotions as they came in, and because I observed them, they left, and the void of anxiety was filled with a peaceful and grounded feeling. It was very similar to the feeling I had when I met my majestic woman; as if I understood everything that was my life as it was in this very moment—as it was meant to be.

I have to say that I was somewhat shocked to have a wave of anxiety come in like that and for it not to stay with me, consuming my every thought and cell in my body and hijacking the day. In fact, the whole experience took place in less than five minutes. I took a deep, long breath and plunged into the ocean, thanking her for the healing moment I had just experienced.

I was alone in the ocean for close to 30 minutes before Ari came to join me from the house. I can't recall feeling as calm as I was in that moment in a long, long time. As I floated along in the waves, I had an epiphany—a flash of clarity about all of the moments that had brought me to this one.

It wasn't as simple as thinking, *Wow, every moment in my life brought me to this book*, though that was a true statement. It was as if me thinking about these things came in small packets of information that downloaded, and they arrived in four categories:

Surrender, observation, curiosity, and love.

I was made acutely aware that I had indeed **surrendered** my childhood, my suffering, and my pain. Not just once, but something I do every day. It was through working with Anna that I learned how to **observe** myself and my triggers in the moment. Only then was I able to change my thoughts and heal my body. Anna helped me to stop judging and hating on myself for how I felt or didn't feel. Together, she and I then got **curious** about my pain, curious about my feelings, and it was through this curiosity that my inner child felt safe enough to tell her story. Healing my inner child was *the* source of my true healing. And in the end, I was able to not only **love** myself, broken and a mess, but I also began loving my friends and family more than ever before.

I cried a small tear of joy as Mother Ocean engulfed me in her unconditional love that day in Florida. I felt my body healing as I was in true surrender; I wasn't trying to control any outcome. I felt in flow and connected to what I have been telling my clients for years:

Life is happening *for* you, not *to* you!

This epiphany in the ocean was a big moment for me, and as the Universe does to all of us, it came at a time I needed it the most. Writing a book was the most difficult thing I had ever done. I cannot even tell you how many times I almost gave up, feeling so overwhelmed by the whole process. I am sure you can identify with me on this; I have shared so many vulnerable parts of me with you, the reader. That is scary! Putting myself out there pushed me right up against so many of my triggers.

I imagined people's responses, thinking the worst: *Who does she think she is, telling her story as if it matters in the grand scheme of the world? There are so many people who had it worse off than her.* In fact, that was one of my greatest fears in writing the book you hold in your hands—that people would say those things about me.

The endorsement phase was the second hardest, the waiting for approval from people I looked up to the most. There was a ton of radio silence during that phase of the process, and boy did I have a headache while I waited to be told my book wasn't good enough to endorse and prayed to get even one positive endorsement.

With each and every trigger I surrendered, I was able to observe my headache for what it was—fear. I got curious, and in the end, I loved myself anyway. I loved myself for writing the book, even if I didn't get a single endorsement. I loved myself for being vulnerable, and I loved myself because I knew I was worthy of it.

I believe that these four pillars are what continue to help me to heal. That moment at the beach reminded me that I already practice these daily, and this process is how I was able to leave my house, go back to work, and have a more meaningful marriage.

As we wrap up this book, let's dive a bit deeper into each of the four pillars and see how you can incorporate them into *your* everyday healing.

SURRENDER

I struggled with this concept for years. I would ask every healer and guru I met the same questions: how do I surrender, and why am I having such a difficult time doing it? I can't say that I ever got the answer I was looking for, or perhaps I was not in the right place to hear it.

During a session with Leonard Jacobson, he looked me dead in the eyes and asked me if I believed in God. I quickly answered yes, but he said, "No, you don't; I can see it in your eyes."

He had me close my eyes and connect to my breath, and after what felt like 20 minutes, he asked me to open them. "What do you feel?" he asked. I didn't know how to answer him, and I felt like I was failing a test.

"I don't feel anything," I answered with massive hesitation, hoping that was the correct answer.

"Good," he said. "You have lost your Ego. I watched it happen on your face while your eyes were closed. *That* is surrender. Do this every day, and you will find your healing, your peace."

"You mean meditate?" I asked. "I do this every day." I felt like I needed to explain myself.

"You don't do it like we just did," he said, "otherwise, you would not have come to me for a session."

I left that session feeling frustrated. Why isn't surrender easier? Why wasn't my meditation practice allowing me to drop my Ego, and what was I doing wrong?

That moment at the beach when the download of my life and healing journey came to me, it became clear as day. You don't surrender once and then things are magically better. You need to surrender every single day. I was doing this; every time I woke up with a headache, I would journal it out. Over time, I gave up trying to change my headache. I gave up trying to force myself to get better. I gave up getting mad at myself that my headache was going to ruin the weekend. I gave up my fear that I was going to have to attend school functions, work meetings, and social gatherings with a headache.

I came to the conclusion that this was my reality, and fighting it wouldn't change a damn thing. I told myself in the moments of week-long migraines that I had done this before, and I could do it again. I gave myself permission to opt out if I needed to, without feeling as if I failed. I was in surrender to my pain.

Most importantly, I celebrated small accomplishments like being able to go to a loud restaurant with a migraine and enjoy time with friends. That may sound terrifying for those of you reading this who are suffering from chronic pain, but at some point in your healing, you too will go out when your pain level is at your usual nine out of ten. Because that is part of the healing: realizing that your pain doesn't have to control your life. It is your fear circuits that are telling you to stay home, not work out, and miss out on life. We *can* live with pain.

I tell you honestly that I don't think I will ever stop surrendering. As we say in the healer's world, *and so it is.*

> *Try this on for size: Make a list of the top ten issues in your life that are causing you physical or emotional pain. All you must do is say the following (out loud, so the Universe can hear you): I surrender my _____.*

> *Then do the work daily. Talk to your pain and talk to yourself about the situation. Allow the feelings you are fighting so hard to keep down to come forward and tell you their story. As I have shared with you in previous chapters, it is the repression of emotions that keeps us unwell because we are not actually experiencing them. Try the journaling techniques I mentioned earlier.*

Write out "Dear headache..." and then get curious. Why are you here?
Are you trying to protect me from something? What do you really want
to tell me?

OBSERVE

Without a doubt, I know that my meditation practice is largely responsible
for how I am able to observe my triggers each day. It is our Ego that gets
in the way of our ability to see ourselves for who we truly are because it is
trying to protect us. That whole Ego dance is a mess, and it's ass-backward.
The mere fact that our Ego thinks we can't handle feeling alone, scared, or
angry is absurd. I am here to tell you we *can* experience negative emotions
and survive.

I would even wager that feeling all of our feelings will bring us closer to
freedom.

Meditation is how we learn to keep our Ego in check; to remind it
that we are the ones driving the bus.
We do this in every moment we are
distracted by thoughts during our
meditation. We simply observe the
thought and then come back to the
mantra or the breath. If we focus on
the thought and trail off, the Ego
wins. So, we gently come back without judgment that we got distracted
in the first place. If we get angry or
frustrated with ourselves during our

In order to heal, we must
feel. If you are afraid to
feel, you need to let your
Ego go. Use meditation
as a method to gently
kick your Ego to the side
where it belongs.

practice, that is the Ego trying to control us all over again! We train the
dragon by coming back to source—to our breath, to our mantra.

In order to heal, we must feel. If you are afraid to feel, you need to let
your Ego go. Use meditation as a method to gently kick your Ego to the
side where it belongs.

CURIOSITY

Judgment is the evil that keeps the world divided. We see it every day on the
news and social media—it is everywhere. However, we often judge others

because we see parts of ourselves we don't like in them. Many people will argue with me on this point.

How can I see myself in a murderer? you might be asking.

To which I say, the same way I can see myself in my mother.

Because we are all expressions of the same energy, and if that is true, then good and evil exist in all of us. We may not all be murderers, but we have evil inside us that we are terrified will come out. We can go around and around on this topic, but what is most important here is that the judgment you hold against yourself is 10 times more hurtful than the judgments others have on you.

Trust me, your inner dialogue is what keeps you up at night, not what your co-worker said to you at lunch.

I was so angry with myself when I was sick. I would say vile things to my face in the mirror. Just like Nate, in the Apple TV series Ted Lasso, when he would spit on his own face in the mirror. Like, *that* angry. Why do we hate on ourselves like Nate and I did? I believe when children are

Observe your inner critic. How do you talk to yourself daily? Then get curious and ask why.

not loved, accepted, and made to feel safe, we turn on ourselves, thinking it was our fault.

It took me almost a year of working with Anna to get *curious* about my inner critic. It was only through this method that I exposed how my inner child was angry with herself as a protection mechanism of survival.

Observe your inner critic. How do you talk to yourself daily? Then get curious and ask why.

LOVE

You have probably heard the age-old saying that you cannot love anyone until you first love yourself. Well, whoever coined this term is a fucking genius because I have found it to be true over and over and over again. When we are unable to love ourselves for our shortcomings—when we see these as failures and not just a small part of who we are—we are living an inauthentic life. To be authentic is to truly know yourself through observation and then to love yourself—for *all* of you. No one is perfect. And what is perfect anyway? Perfect is *not* being happy all the time, it isn't helping everyone else at your own expense, and it surely isn't the absence of negative emotions.

Perfect is you, just as you are in this very moment. Perfect is broken, hurt, in pain, not in pain. Perfect is you when you are sad, perfect is you at your best. Perfect is all of you.

I began to love myself for the first time through, you guessed it, working with Anna. I cried so hard the first time I said the words out loud.

"I do love myself," I told her. "I am proud of myself even when shit is fucked up. Even when I am sick."

"Even when you fail?" she asked.

"Even more when I fail!" I cried, and we both just laughed together.

"Yes, even more when you fail," she said. "Do you know why?"

"Because I need love more in that moment than any other. I need love even more when I feel badly about myself and fear that I am not loveable. I deserve to be loved," I replied, wiping the tears away once again.

We all deserve to be loved, no matter what. No matter what.

> *After you surrender to your life and your feelings, you begin to observe yourself for truly who you are, and you get curious rather than judgmental, I want you to ask yourself how you can love yourself in this very moment. What do you need to feel loved? Do you need to know that even when you fail, you are still a good person? Do you need to know that giving yourself a break is OK?*
>
> *Once you find the answers, remember to communicate to your inner child. How does writing a letter to yourself sound? How about a sticky note on your bathroom mirror: You are loveable, and I love you!*

Thank you for allowing me to share a small part of my life with you. Thank you for reading this. I wish you all the love in the world as you continue your healing path.

Namaste, my dear reader, Namaste.

About Author

Ashley Haseotes is an intuitive energy healer and Chopra Center certified meditation coach as well as the author of *The Unspoken*.

Ashley wrote *The Unspoken* after she healed following a collapse into chronic pain from over working and ignoring built up childhood trauma. People work with Ashley when they are feeling stuck or struggling on their life path, in pain, or going through a major life shift. She is dedicated to helping children and their families heal during and after pediatric cancer through the charity she founded, One Mission.

For more information on Ashley visit her website AshleyHaseotes.com or OneMission.org.

Ashley resides in Massachusetts with her husband and three children.

Resources

The following is a list of resources I've found helpful in my healing journey: healers, meditations, books, and organizations. They are all profound in their own rights and I know you'll find something for you here.

Ashley Haseotes
https://www.veda-healing.org

Nicole Sachs
https://www.thecureforchronicpain.com

Dr. Joe Dispenza
https://drjoedispenza.com

Dr. Brian Weiss
https://www.brianweiss.com

Rob Wergin
https://robwergin.com

HEAL
https://www.healdocumentary.com

Lisa Campion
https://lisacampion.com

Jack Kornfield
After Ecstasy, then Laundry

Glennon Doyle
Untamed

Dr. Sarno
Read all of his books!

Jodi Picoult
My Sister's Keeper

Curable App
https://www.curablehealth.com

Other Websites:
www.traumahealing.org
www.ifs-institute.com
www.aedpinstitute.org
www.sensorimotorpsychotherapy.org
www.ppdassociation.org/directory
https://www.cnvc.org
https://khironclinics.com
https://www.painpsychologycenter.com